Michael Reed Gach

GREATER ENERGY
AT YOUR FINGERTIPS

How To Easily Increase Your Vitality
In Ten Minutes

CELESTIAL ARTS
Berkeley, California

Acknowledgments

To Elizabeth Rosner whose writing talents transformed this book and to Kathy Moring whose valuable administrative skills provide a foundation for the Acupressure Institute's growth.

Library of Congress Cataloging-in-Publication Data:

Gach, Michael Reed.
  Greater energy at your fingertips.

  Bibliography: p.
  Includes index. 1. Exercise.   2. Vitality.   I. Title.
  RA781.G33 1986   613.7'1   86-11784
  ISBN: 0-89087-473-5

Manufactured in the United States of America

First Printing, 1986

          87   88   89   90   —   5   4   3   2   1

CELESTIALARTS
P.O. Box 7327
Berkeley, California 94707

Cover photography:
  Prismatic Despersions by Barbara Dorsey
Cover and book design by Nancy Austin
Interior photography by David Blankenhorn
Typography by HMS Typography

TABLE OF CONTENTS

INTRODUCTION

GREATER ENERGY AT YOUR FINGERTIPS is simple and easy to do, yet it is also powerful and effective. It involves positive thinking, a balanced natural foods diet, self-acupressure and daily exercises for stress reduction and self-improvement. Increased effectiveness is the result of combining these holistic health promotion practices into a comprehensive system for self-treatment. These classical exercises and acupressure techniques have survived over 5,000 years of experimental development in China. They have proved to be valuable, natural methods of preventing illness and building better health. They relax muscular tension, improve circulation and breathing, and balance the vital life energy of the body.

The Greater Energy system is designed to improve the general health and vigor of *all* people, young and old. The exercises and points are so simple that anyone can learn them. They are moderate enough to suit a weak person, yet the movements can be extended to challenge a strong one by increasing the practice time.

*Marc Duke, Acupuncture, Pyramid House, 1972: 20-21.

Our Vital Life Force

Tests done with highly developed technological equipment have verified that there is a profound system of human electrical energy that circulates through all the tissues and internal organs of the body, penetrating every living cell. We in the West are only beginning to appreciate the importance of this life energy, called *chi* in China, *prana* in East India, and *ki* in Japan.

This essential human life force travels through the body along distinct pathways called *meridians*. Along the meridians are key *points* where you can tap into and affect the energy flow (note that these are the meridians and points of acupuncture and acupressure—the systems of Oriental health care). These points can be located and measured scientifically.*

The points are the places where circulation tends to get blocked or stagnated, thus preventing a balanced flow of fluids through the body. The Greater Energy exercises and acupressure techniques are designed to awaken our energy, release tension, and balance the vital systems of the body. When the energy flows smoothly and freely, all the organs and tissues are nourished, and a feeling of harmony and well-being is restored. This can be accomplished with regular practice of the exercises in this book.

The Origins of Disease

In traditional Oriental health care it is said that diseases are all initially caused by tension and stress, that is, by "dis-ease," a lack of ease. When muscular tension accumulates around the points, it blocks our energy from flowing properly.

The circulation of the blood is also impeded, so that the area cannot properly receive new nutrients and expel its waste products. This stagnation and toxicity creates the kind of internal environment in which various ailments can develop.

No matter what level of health you experience, tension and stress always contribute to health problems. For example, fatigue, insomnia, indigestion, and high blood pressure are all related to and worsened by stress.

Creating Vibrant Health

Since the first stages of diseases are associated with tension and toxicity, it is to our advantage to work on our physical tensions, imbalances, and blockages when they are at the least developed stage, before they have caused damage to the internal organs. Greater Energy exercises enable us to do exactly that—to reduce or eliminate tensions before they have developed

into illnesses. This is known as preventative health care.

The great sages of the East were masters of preventative health care. A number of the movements, acupressure points, and breathing techniques that they used are included in the Greater Energy exercises. Each exercise naturally and effectively stretches and presses certain nerves, muscles, points, and meridians. This releases tension and helps eliminate toxins, enabling the energy to circulate freely.

As a result, the body's normal functions are balanced by stimulating our natural self-regulating healing mechanisms. Thus, by using certain key acupressure points along with therapeutic breathing, we can generate greater energy. These highly developed methods of preventative health care also contribute to a more expanded or developed state, known as *vibrant health*.

Vibrant health is more than simply the absence of disease, pain, or fatigue. It is a feeling of energy, flexibility, strength, wholeness, and aliveness. A vibrantly healthy person feels good, rather than "okay," or just "not bad." We can begin to create this state of vibrant health for ourselves through daily practice of the Greater Energy exercises.

The Importance of Exercise

The amount and kind of exercise you do makes a tremendous difference in your health. Exercise is one of the most powerful ways we have of creating a healthy body free from tension, pain, and disease. It is also one of the most effective methods of relieving ailments related to stress and tension.

Exercise is central to good health. Doctors, physical therapists, and other health care professionals all over the world recognize the importance of regular exercise for maintaining and improving health.

The body must be used in order to function properly and remain healthy. Some of us, however, have practically stopped using our bodies. The availability of cars, television, and other machines has changed people's lifestyles; these modern conveniences can result in an unhealthy *under-use* of the body. Daily chores such as chopping wood and washing clothes have been either eliminated or taken over by machines. As a result, people have become more sedentary. We need to make a special effort to make exercise a regular part of our lives.

The exercises in this book can work wonders in relieving fatigue and tension. Other common disorders caused or accentuated by stress also respond positively to regular exercise. If you've never exercised regularly, now is the time to try it and experience the benefits for yourself.

Exercise for Older People

The Greater Energy exercises are especially suitable for senior people. When practiced without strain, in moderation, the slow, rhythmic movements enable older people to feel younger, to regain strength and flexibility.

The human body, like a machine, will last longer if used properly and kept in good condition. Thus, exercise is a means of preserving youth–by keeping the physical body in shape.

Age, of course, is not only a matter of years, but also of one's outlook on life. The Greater Energy exercises and acupressure points also help create emotional balance and a calm, relaxed state of mind, and are conducive to a positive outlook on life. Greater Energy methods are easy and satisfying for older people to learn and practice. They can be done by anyone with minimum physical ability. No matter what condition you're in you can benefit from this easy self-care system.

Benefits

The Greater Energy exercise system is designed to improve the overall condition of the body. By practicing the exercises in this book, you can take responsibility not only for your general health, you can also work towards creating *vibrant* health.

The movements revitalize the entire body. This positive influence spills over into other aspects of our lives; you can use the exercises to improve your condition on all levels–physical, emotional, mental, and spiritual–since they are directly inter-connected. If you feel good physically, you are more likely to feel good emotionally. For, when our energy is circulating properly, we have a greater sense of well-being, health, and vitality.

Just the physical benefits, however, are many. The exercises increase the intake of oxygen, energy, and improve the circulation of the blood. The slow, even, gradual movements, together with proper breathing and relaxation, benefit the cardio-vascular and other body systems, and improve the functioning of the internal organs.

For example, the *nervous system* benefits from the Greater Energy exercises. It regulates the other systems of the body and is the means by which we perceive our environment. These exercises benefit the nervous system, first, by balancing the two sides of the brain, which perform different but complementary functions, and second, by stretching and releasing tension in the spine. Since the nervous impulses running between the brain and all parts of the body flow through the central nerve cord in the spine, the strength and flexibility of the spine is key to the state of the nervous system.

The *respiratory system* is strengthened by the deep, quiet, long breathing of these exercises. They also relax tensions in the entire chest and fully oxygenate the lungs.

As you breathe deeply, the contraction and expansion of the diaphragm rhythmically massages the internal digestive organs, including the liver, gall bladder, stomach, spleen, pancreas, and the large and small intestines. This gentle massage helps

these organs to function properly, thus strengthening the *digestive system* as a whole.

The *circulatory system* is helped by any exercise. The physical movements and exertion of the exercise cause the heart to beat faster. It pumps more blood to nourish the muscles which are working in the exercise.

The *urinary and reproductive systems* also benefit from the practice of Greater Energy exercises. Movements of the waist, pelvis, and abdomen release pelvic tensions. This allows the blood and *chi* to circulate into the area for balancing the functions of the urinary and reproductive organs.

Do not mistake the therapeutics of exercise as being a form of medicine. Exercise is not used like a pill to cure an illness, although some conditions do respond positively to exercise therapeutics. The Greater Energy exercise system is meant for maintaining and building health. The system works best with regular practice over a period of time. Good health can be cultivated and sustained through the practice of these exercises.

In practicing the Greater Energy exercises each individual is an artist. Each person will develop a personal way of doing the exercises. The basic principles are maintained, yet the individual expression of them varies slightly from person to person. Make these exercises your own. Use them to express yourself, to get more fully in touch with your body, and to create the experience of vibrant health for yourself.

I

Foundations for Self-Improvement

FOUNDATIONS FOR SELF-IMPROVEMENT

IN ORDER TO increase your energy and participate in life as fully as possible, you must cultivate an awareness of your body. Your body is constantly sending out a flow of thoughts and feelings which are messages for you to receive and act upon. For instance, when your shoulders become tense, it's a signal to change. You might need to get away from what you are doing, or from your immediate environment. You may only need to change the position of your body; just shrugging your shoulders and taking a deep breath might relax them.

If you concentrate on developing your awareness, you can attune yourself to the inner mechanisms of your body. This awareness of trusting your feelings and body signals is vital for having greater energy. The development of body awareness takes real work on your part and involves the following elements:

- Intuition
- Mental Attitudes
- Daily Physical Exercise
- Relaxation for Greater Energy
- Balancing Pain and the Emotions through the Breath
- Awareness in Daily Life

Trusting Your Intuition

One way to develop greater energy is to cultivate a connection with your own inner voice. This communication with your inner self is called "the teacher within." The teacher within is the most valuable source of constant information and wisdom for knowing at any given moment what your body needs to obtain greater energy. It is the most profound teacher you will ever find in terms of receiving inner guidance.

If you know how to listen to the signals of your body, you are better equipped to handle your self development and improvement. One of the first steps is to know and accept the condition of your body. If you know where you are stiff, and you know exercises for stretching out that part of the body, then your awareness of that stiffness becomes a clue for you to act upon. If you are aware that your inner voices are clues to guide you, and you act upon your intuitive thoughts, then you will be your own teacher and develop your energy at an amazing pace.

Through practicing the Greater Energy exercises in this book, you will learn a great deal about yourself. The thoughts that arise during the exercises may result in clearer insights about yourself. As body therapy, these self-help techniques strengthen your growth potential by developing an awareness of the inner mechanisms of the body. This self-awareness enables you to utilize your body for being most effective in the world.

By consciously practicing with an awareness of your body, you can gain more strength and personal power. The first step is to trust yourself. This trust of your own feelings, responses, actions, needs, etc., forms a foundation for all other relationships in life. The more you experience these relationships with an open mind, the more you will be able to trust, and also respond openly. Positive relationships, without a doubt, will add greater energy to your life.

Attitudes:
Toward Positive Thinking

Your attitude strongly affects how much energy you have. It's important to be aware of what your attitude is expressing. A negative or judgmental attitude can hinder your experience by blocking off the positive aspects that surround you. When you let go of that rigidity or negativity, you can regain a clarity in the present moment. Your presence in the here and now can naturally enable you to have greater energy, especially when you complement positive thinking with some of the Greater Energy exercises.

A wide range of attitudes may surface while doing the exercises in this book. There are two extremes to this range. One is negative, where exercise becomes a chore. It's frustrating when you are stiff and really do not want to do it. But there is also a positive attitude where it is fun, when it is a joy and a challenge to move and stretch. With a positive attitude you can go deeper and deeper inside yourself. Close your eyes so that you are not distracted, and pay closer attention to what you are feeling.

The "will to become" is an important drive for improving the quality of one's life. It enables you to contact the place within you where you want to have greater energy, and live a deeper, fuller life. Develop this kind of attitude as you practice the exercises in this book. Put your heart into whatever you do.

Daily Physical Exercise

Daily movement and stretching are important to keep your muscles and joints loose, as is aerobic exercise such as swimming, bicycle riding, or brisk walking to stimulate deep breathing, sweating, and increased circulation. Each Greater Energy exercise stimulates and affects different systems of the body; each influences certain endocrine glands, nerves, muscles, organs, and meridians.

Your posture relates to how you feel, and is an expression of what your body needs. Becoming aware of how you carry your body is an important Greater Energy goal. This awareness not only enhances the effectiveness of the exercise routines, but of all your pursuits in life.

There is a process that you go through with each exercise. When you first learn a new exercise, it is just a technique. This is the first stage of grasping the mechanical aspects of the exercise.

In the second stage you still have to concentrate on the mechanics of the exercise, but at the same time you can become more aware of yourself through the dynamics of the movement. From a set of mechanical techniques, the exercise becomes a more refined movement, smooth and graceful, like a dance.

The third stage progressively develops as you begin to master the exercise or pose. At this point, the exercise becomes a meditation where you no longer have to concentrate on what you are doing, but can feel the energy and totally experience the entire movement.

Always tune into your body when you practice the exercises. This is best accomplished by simply closing your eyes, and turning your attention to the feelings in your body. Do the exercises without strain. Let your body stretch as far as it wants to go, trusting your own judgment. In practicing, it is essential to trust your own limitations. Remember that your pace will vary, depending on the circumstances at any particular time. Be flexible and recognize that you will discover the pace that's right for you. We all have different needs and abilities.

Using Relaxation for Greater Energy

The art of relieving tension is an important aspect of the Greater Energy exercises. Instinctively, we use our hands to hold areas where there is pain and pressure, to help release the knots of tension. It's interesting to note that tension tends to collect around the acupressure points. Actually, this is how you locate the points: by feeling for and holding the places where you are tight. Often it is important to hold these points during or after an exercise in order to help release that area. In practicing the exercises, you can learn to adjust your hands and hold the blocked areas. Once your fingertips are directly on the tense area and your body position is comfortable, patiently keep your body still for a minute. In this way you can deeply but gently work on releasing your tensions.

Sometimes after you do an exercise, you may get lightheaded, or feel new sensations moving through your body. This is what happens when the acupressure points begin to release. The energy that was bound up as tension inside the point is now able to circulate throughout the body. This is the most important time to let yourself deeply relax, in order to enable the released energy to distribute throughout the body and be utilized for increasing your vitality. Through the development of an awareness of your body, positive thinking, and the use of acupressure, the path to greater energy unfolds.

Balancing Pain and the Emotions Through the Breath

If you push yourself too far, you will reach a point where an exercise may become painful. What you want to do is stretch to the point where you feel some degree of both pain and pleasure. If you only feel pain doing an exercise, this is an indication that you are pushing yourself too hard. You should release a little so that you still feel the stretch, but the position is comfortable. Always focus on your breath when you do feel pain. Imagine you are breathing into and out of the painful stretch. Long, deep breathing is a key for opening up tightness in the nerves and muscles.

The breath is the key to self-awareness and greater energy. When your breath is shallow, you may become fatigued and lack control of your emotions. If you increase the capacity of your breath, making it long, deep, and gentle, you can gain an abundance of energy and full aware-ness. But many times, when some part of you is blocked, it is difficult to breathe fully. It might be due to a number of things: constriction in the chest due to emotional pain or anxiety; a great deal of grief or sadness; holding onto an unfulfilled expectation; or it might be due to a physical disability.

Whatever the cause may be, difficult breathing relates to some kind of blockage and eventually leads to exhaustion. The purpose of tuning into your body is to discover the inner language of these body expressions. The more aware you can become of yourself, all parts of yourself, the more alive you will be to experience the wonders in life.

Greater Energy in Daily Life

A special beauty and delight comes in applying the Greater Energy program to your daily life. Although the exercises have a cumulative effect when done regularly, they can also be used spontaneously, whenever you want or need them, at any time. At work, for example, you may discover through your growing awareness that the way you hold your body creates tension. You can then use the acupres-sure points and easy stretches to release the blockages, and learn new ways of sitting or standing that don't cause tension.

If you go jogging or running, you can use some Greater Energy exercises. You can practice deep breathing, you can hold points, you can improve your posture, and you can stretch tight, tired muscles. Have fun creatively using the Greater Energy program in your daily life.

II

Acupressure Tonic Points

ACUPRESSURE TONIC POINTS

THERE ARE SPECIAL acupressure points that effectively strengthen the whole system of the body and thereby increase vitality. By stimulating each of these points daily, you can improve your overall condition and obtain greater energy for whatever you choose to do.

Each tonic point is important for both improving circulation and fortifying various internal organs and vital systems of the body. For instance, there are several points which tone and strengthen the condition of the muscles. Athletes, builders, and travelers have used these points successfully for thousands of years in the Orient to increase their endurance and stamina. There is another set of points along the back which restores the condition of the general nervous system. There are other tonic points for the empathic system, which improve circulation and help detoxify the system; points for the endocrine system which stimulate the glands to function properly; points for the brain that improve memory and the ability to concentrate; and other special tonic points in the abdomen which improve the condition of many internal organs

and therefore strengthen the whole body.

This chapter illustrates and describes how to locate each tonic point anatomically. You will learn how best to press these points on yourself, and also how to press the points on others. Lastly, you will gain an understanding of the uses and benefits of each point for increased vitality and radiant health.

How Acupressure Works to Increase Energy

Several theories exist to explain how acupressure works to build vitality, strength and endurance. One of the main physiological benefits of acupressure is the improvement of circulation. Acupressure releases muscular tension, enabling the blood to flow freely. An increase of circulation also brings more oxygen and other nutrients to affected areas. This increases your overall energy as well as resistance to illness, and promotes a longer life. When our blood and energy are circulating properly, we have a greater sense of harmony, health, and well-being.

Acupressure and acupuncture stimulate the pituitary gland to release endorphins. These natural neurochemicals manufactured within the body function to inhibit pain, promote healing, heighten morale, self-esteem, and increase our energy.

Acupressure releases muscular tension and creates an "alpha-wave" response in the brain. This state of deep relaxation allows for increased circulation, which removes toxins from the body and enables us to increase our vitality and sense of general well-being.

Since the first stages of disease are associated with tension and toxicity, it is to our advantage to work on our physical tensions when they are at the least developed stage, before they have caused damage to the internal organs. Acupressure enables us to do exactly that—to reduce or eliminate tensions before they develop into illness. It is a preventative health care practice which contributes to the development of vibrant health.

Locating Acupressure Points

Many of the primary acupressure points for boosting your energy are located in muscular areas. Tension often accumulates around these points, resulting in depression, sluggishness, or fatigue. Sometimes the area is quite large and covers major muscles, particularly around the back and shoulders. You can actually locate a point by feeling for this tension, which is usually in the form of a *tight muscular band, cord,* or *knot* surrounding the point.

Often a point is indicated by some degree of soreness upon pressure. Look for a spot approximately the size of a dime located near the center of tight areas. It will feel sore when pressure is applied. If there is extreme (or an increase in) sensitivity or pain, gradually decrease the pressure until a balance is achieved between pain and pleasure.

Soreness upon pressure or tension surrounding a point indicates a blockage. Several minutes of firm finger pressure on these specific points strongly helps to release blockages and rebalance the body.

Sometimes an acupressure point is not sore when pressed or is not found in an area where muscular tension forms. Many of these acupressure points are located in anatomically important locations, such as joints or bone depressions. In this case, there will usually be a small dip or hollow in which the point can be found.

The more exactly you stimulate the correct point, the stronger the effect will be. First, look carefully at the photographs accompanying the points and then try to find them on your own body. These points will be either sensitive or sore upon pressure. Second, read the text describing the location of the points. To be sure of finding the right acupressure point, locate the most sensitive spot in the area illustrated.

The following is a self-acupressure routine that uses some of the most powerful acupressure points of the body. For best results, press these points while lying down in a relaxed, comfortable position. Close your eyes and hold the points for one or two minutes, breathing deeply into your abdomen; the breathing helps open the flow of energy through the meridians and points. Visualize the energy in the points and feel the circulation of this energy throughout your whole body. Relaxation and a feeling of well-being will emerge the more you practice doing self-acupressure as a daily routine.

The right amount of pressure is variable from person to person and point to point. The pressure should be gentle but firm, so that you feel a balance between pain and pleasure.

Basically, people with more developed muscles require deeper pressure, so that men often need more firm, deep pressure and women a lighter pressure.

Sometimes when you are holding a point, it will cause a pain in another part of the body. This is known as "referred pain" which indicates that the two areas are related. Note where these extra sore places are and hold those spots at the same time to release their blockages as well.

Breathe into the points and allow yourself to relax so that the energy can circulate. Each point, except for those on the midline of the body, is bilateral, that is, there is one on each side of the body. Hold the points on both sides for a complete release.

"Sea of Energy"
Conception Vessel 6 (CV6)*

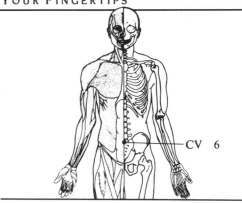

CV 6

This tonic point (often referred to as the "hara") is the most important self-acupressure point for the development of energy and physical power. For this reason, most martial arts teach how to concentrate on this Sea of Energy for obtaining greater strength and balance. This point tonifies the abdominal muscles, intestines, and helps to fortify the uro-reproductive system. Structurally, the Chinese consider this point to be the center of gravity in the body; if two diagonal lines were drawn across the body with the arms and legs extended, the lines would cross at this vital point.

Location: The exact point is located three finger-widths below the navel (belly button) and one to two inches deep inside the abdomen.

These names and numbers refer to the acupuncture/acupressure point system of the body.

Self-Help:
1. Place one of your fists over the point between your pubic bone and your navel.
2. Place the palm of your hand over your fist.
3. Gently lie down on your stomach with your hands in this position.
4. Close your eyes and breathe slowly—long, deep breaths for two minutes.
5. Completely relax with your hands by your sides, your palms facing up and your eyes closed for two more minutes.

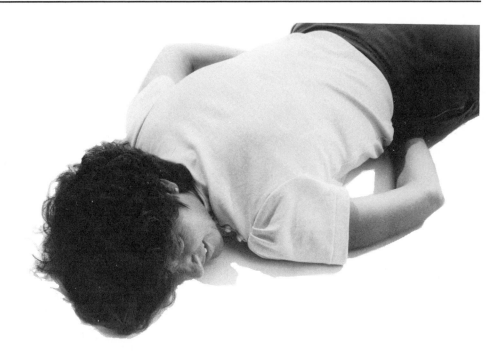

For Helping Others:

1. Have the recipient lie down on his/her back with knees bent, feet shoulder-width apart and flat on the ground.
2. Place your fingers of both your hands on the center of the recipient's lower belly. Gradually, very gradually, apply pressure, taking one full minute to slowly descend one inch into the abdomen.†
3. Hold at this depth for two minutes while you encourage the recipient to breathe deeply into your fingertips.
4. Gradually release the pressure.

†Note of caution: Apply less pressure to people who are weak or sick, more pressure to those who are athletic and healthy. In general, apply less pressure and hold for less time when you do not know the full extent of a person's condition. If a person has a disease of any type, consult a qualified holistic health professional with experience in acupressure.

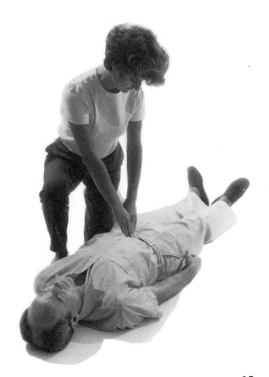

13

"Sea of Vitality"
Bladder 23 and 47 (B23, B47)

These pressure points in the lower back are helpful for improving the overall condition of the body. Steady, firm pressure (just enough pressure to "hurt good") on these points helps to tonify the reproductive system, rejuvenate the internal organs, and relieve pain associated with lower back problems.*

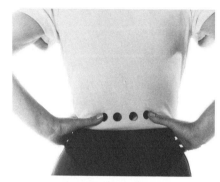

---

*Note of caution: Always use common sense when using the pressure points. Do not press on disintegrating disc problems and fractured or broken bones. A few minutes of stationary, light touch instead of pressure can also be very healing.

Location: The Sea of Vitality points are located in the lower back (between the second and third vertebrae), a few inches out (laterally) from the spine at the level of the waist. They can be found by pressing the outer edge of the large vertical muscles (the muscles that run alongside the spine) in toward the center of the vertebrae. This inward pressure will stimulate both the sets (inner and outer) of points. Use either your thumbs or the heel of your hand to stimulate one side at a time or both sides at once.

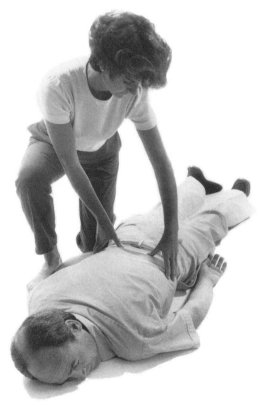

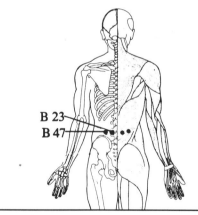

B 23
B 47

For Helping Others:
1. Have recipient lie on his/her stomach. Straddle the body or kneel to one side.
2. Bend over and use the backs of your fists in a slow rocking motion to gradually press the Sea of Vitality points.

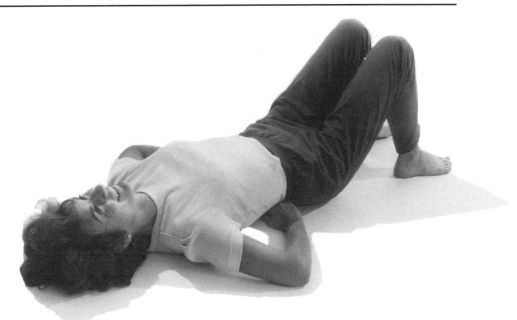

Self-Help:
1. Lie down on your back with your fists underneath your lower back.
2. Position your hands so that your knuckles are pressing into the thick, rope-like muscles in your lower back.
3. Close your eyes. Concentrate on breathing deeply into your lower back. Continue to hold while breathing deeply for two minutes. Beginners should start with one minute and increase the time slowly.
4. Optional: A couple of tennis balls instead of your fists under the lower back often works well.

"Three Mile Point"
Stomach 36 (St 36)

On the outside of the leg, just below the knee, is one of the most effective acupressure points for counteracting fatigue. This instant energy point is one of the most famous acupressure points known throughout China and Japan. Firm pressure on the Three Mile Point immediately fortifies the body with renewed energy. It helps to tone and strengthen the major muscle groups enabling one to have greater endurance.

Athletes in strenuous leg-oriented sports, especially soccer, basketball, and football players, as well as runners, bicycle riders, backpackers, skiers, and long-distance hikers have successfully used this tonic point to ease physical fatigue and increase stamina.

Location: To find the exact point on yourself, measure four finger-widths below your knee cap. Place your fingertips one finger-width outside of your shin bone. If you are on the correct spot, a muscle should pop out as you flex your foot up and down.

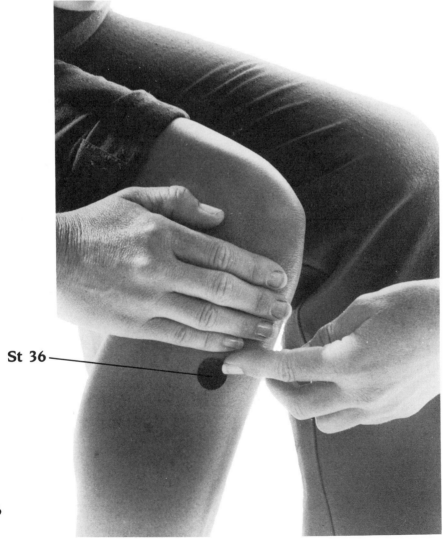

St 36

Self-Help: A heel massage is one of the most effective methods for stimulating this point on yourself.

1. Place your right heel on the Three Mile Point of your left leg and briskly rub it for one minute.
2. Do the same on the other side.

For Helping Others: To be most effective, firm pressure is required on the Three Mile Point. The recipient can be sitting in a chair or lying on his/her back with knees bent and feet on the floor. Use your thumbs to press on both sides simultaneously.

1. Feel for the muscle that runs one inch outside and parallel to the shin (tibia) bone.
2. Position your thumbs four finger-widths below the knee caps, on the outer portion of this muscle. With your elbows outward, use your body weight to firmly press the point in toward the shin bone at a 90 degree angle from the surface of the skin.
3. Lean into the point firmly for two minutes, as both you and your partner breathe deeply together.

"Upper Vitality Point"
Large Intestine 10 (LI 10)

If you ever feel tired or depressed, try pressing this forearm point. The point will often be sore, especially when you are feeling low or when your colon is congested. This is a great tonic point to press for developing vitality in the upper portion of your body. Try stimulating this point for one minute each on both arms when you get up in the morning or as a break at work along with the "Upholding Heaven with the Two Hands" deep breathing exercise (see p. 62). They work together as instant energy boosters.

Location: To find this point, first bend your arm to form a crease at the elbow joint. The point is located one inch toward your hand from the end of this crease, on a muscle. When you flex your hand back and forth while holding the point with your other hand, you should feel that muscle pop out if you are on the correct spot.

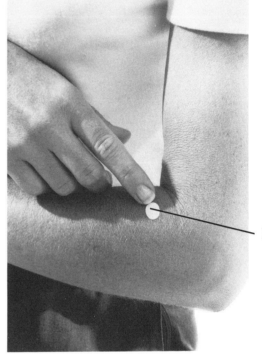

LI 10

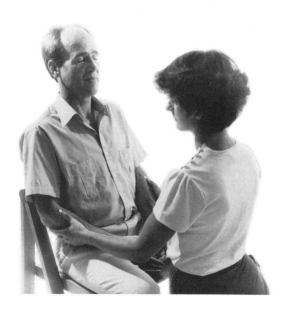

Self-Help:
1. Firmly massage across the forearm muscle on the outside of your arm using your fingers or your thumb.
2. Another way to stimulate the Upper Vitality Point is to firmly hold the point while you rotate your hand on your wrist several times in each direction.

For Helping Others:
1. Have the person close his/her eyes. Encourage him/her to breathe very deeply through the nose.
2. Press the Upper Vitality Point on both sides at the same time and hold for two minutes. Remember that this point is often very tender. The amount of pressure will vary from person to person and should "hurt good," a fine balance between pain and pleasure.

"Outer Gate"
Triple Warmer 5 (TW 5)

This pressure point helps to balance and strengthen the whole body, especially the elasticity of the skin and the tone of the muscles. Firm pressure on this point is also helpful for tightness or pain in the shoulders when used in conjunction with acupressure massage, Shiatsu, or Jin Shin acupressure directly on the shoulders themselves. As an important tonic point, the Outer Gate has been traditionally used for rheumatism, tendonitis, wrist pain, colds and flus.

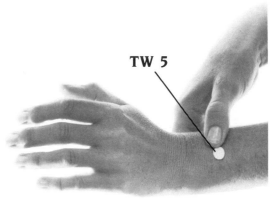

TW 5

Location: To find the Outer Gate, first flex your hand backward. The point is on the outside of the forearm, two finger-widths (approximately 1½ inches) from the wrist crease. Press in firmly between the forearm bones (radius and ulna).

Self-Help: The Outer Gate requires firm, prolonged pressure for best results. You can use either your thumbs or your fingers to stimulate the point, whatever is easier.

1. To get firm pressure, wrap your hand around the wrist (1½ inches from the crease) using both your fingers and thumb to clamp into the outside and inside of your wrist.
2. Hold this point firmly on each arm.

For Helping Others:
1. Grasp hold of recipient's wrists, placing your thumbs on the Outer Gate and using your fingers to wrap around the wrist.
2. Gradually press into the points, and encourage the recipient to breathe deeply for one or two minutes.

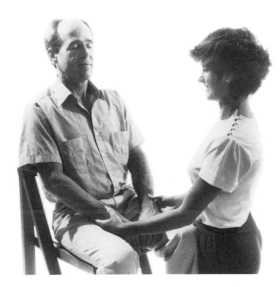

"Bigger Stream"
Kidney 3 (K 3)

This point on the inside of the ankle helps to balance the kidney meridian. In traditional Chinese Medicine the kidneys function as the body's energy storage tanks, gathering a surplus of energy and storing it to be used when needed. For this reason, the kidneys are responsible for developing stamina. This in turn greatly influences the condition of the *chi* or life energy, which affects the overall functions of the body. If the kidneys are strong and balanced, a person will have an abundance of vital energy.

The Bigger Stream more specifically promotes relaxation and has been traditionally used for swollen feet, insomnia, and general fatigue. The uro-genital organs especially benefit from this point. It is also used to balance both an excess or lack of sexual desire when used in conjunction with the Sea of Vitality point in the lower back. Sensitivity to cold, ringing in the ears, semen leakage, swollen ankles, backaches, and menstrual irregularity are some of the traditional indications for using this ankle point.

Location: To find the Bigger Stream point, press the spot midway between the inside of your ankle bone and your achilles tendon in back of your ankle. Press in firmly, angling your pressure in the direction underneath your inner ankle bone.

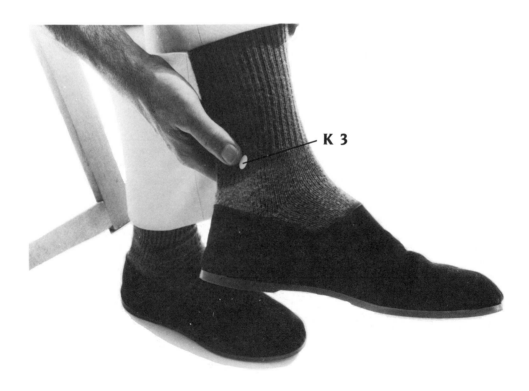

K 3

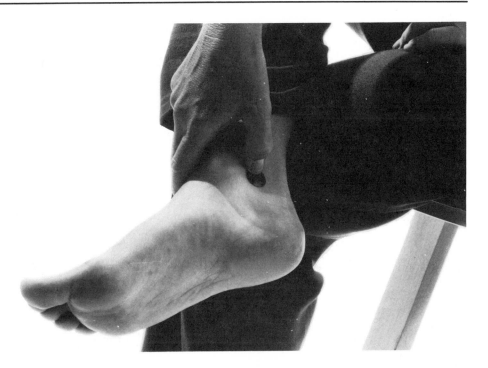

Self-Help: This is a good point to hold while sitting cross-legged in a chair.

1. Grasp your ankle, placing your thumb on the point with your fingers wrapped around the front of your ankle. Position your foot so that the ankle can relax.
2. Hold the point firmly for three minutes or until a pulse can be felt, indicating that energy is moving through the point.

For Helping Others:

1. With the recipient lying down in a prone position, place your thumbs on the Bigger Stream Points, using your other fingers on the outside of the ankle to squeeze in between the ankle bone and the achilles tendon.
2. Hold for one or two minutes, leaning your body weight into your hands.
3. Breathe deeply with your partner for one or two minutes.

"Heavenly Rejuvenation"
Triple Warmer 15 (TW 15)

Chronic shoulder tension, a common condition where contracted muscles are constantly working, is draining to the whole system. This tightness decreases circulation, a blockage that eventually contributes to sluggishness, lethargy, fatigue and even tension headaches. Finger pressure on this point has traditionally been used for nervous tension, stiff neck, increasing resistance to colds and flus, reducing fevers, high blood pressure, and shoulder pain.

TW 15

Location: First locate the spot on the tops of the shoulders that is midway between the outside of the base of your neck and the outside of your shoulders. The Heavenly Rejuvenation Point is located one-half inch directly below this point from the tops of the shoulders.

Self-Help:
1. Reach your right hand over your left shoulder, curving your fingers to hook onto the (trapezius) muscle on the top of your shoulders.
2. Slowly rake your fingers over the muscle to firmly stretch it as your hand continues to slide diagonally across the front of your body.
3. Alternate for each side and continue for one or two minutes.

For Fatigue After Work:
1. Lie on your back with your knees bent, feet flat on the floor.
2. As you deeply inhale, raise your arms and arch your pelvis upward to distribute the weight of your body onto the Heavenly Rejuvenation Points.
3. Exhale and relax down.
4. Continue for one to two minutes with your eyes closed. Follow this exercise with a few Greater Energy breathing exercises.

For Helping Others:
1. Stand behind the recipient who is seated in a chair and rest your fingers on the tops of his/her shoulders.
2. Using your thumbs, feel for a marble of tension above and just outside of the tip of the shoulder blade.
3. Massage the Heavenly Rejuvenation Points with your thumbs. Always remember to slowly increase the pressure, and hold for two minutes as you encourage deep breathing.
4. Gradually release the point.

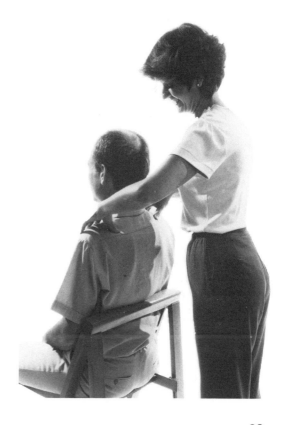

"Third Eye Point"

A few minutes of concentration on this point while lightly touching it with your eyes closed and breathing deeper than you normally breathe, can give you a lift of energy for enhancing your whole day.

The Third Eye Point is a glandular tonic. Light pressure as well as concentrating at this point between the eyebrows stimulates and balances the endocrine system via the pituitary gland. This point has traditionally been used for relieving hay fever, headaches, ulcer pain, eye strain and indigestion.

Location: The Third Eye Point is located directly between your eyebrows, in the indentation where the bridge of your nose meets the lower center ridge of your forehead. Use light pressure or just simply touch the point with your middle finger as you focus all of your attention where you are touching between your brows.

Self-Help: You can gain greater energy simply by meditating at the Third Eye Point.

1. Sit with your spine straight, eyes closed, chin slightly tilted down. Concentrate on your Third Eye Point between your eyebrows.
2. Bring your palms together, and use your middle and index fingertips to lightly touch the Third Eye Point.
3. Take several long, slow, deep breaths as you concentrate on the Third Eye Point for two or three minutes.

Extra Special Energy Boost: Give someone you love a wonderful, uplifting experience. Ask your friend or partner to close his/her eyes for a minute. Position yourself as close as you can, and place your hands over the back of your partner's head. Kiss the Third Eye Point, creating a firm suction with your lips for one to three minutes. Giving this energy boost will uplift and increase the vitality of both people involved.

III

Guidelines for Practicing the Greater Energy Exercises

GUIDELINES FOR PRACTICING THE GREATER ENERGY EXERCISES

- Breathe deeply and slowly with the movement of each exercise;

- Let your movements flow smoothly, gracefully, rhythmically;

- Be aware of your body and your posture;

- Maintain a here and now presence of mind; be calm and alert;

- Practice regularly: cultivate self-discipline.

Breathing: The Key to Vitality

Breathing exercises are invaluable for health.* Proper breathing involves the belly as well as the chest. It is deep, smooth, slow, and relaxed. Your lungs can fully expand when you allow your belly to move with your breath.

This kind of breathing is known (in Japanese) as *hara* breathing. The hara is an important energy center located about two inches below your navel, in the center of the abdomen. This profoundly therapeutic way of breath-

---

See the section in "Breathing Techniques" on page 79 for more information on this important subject.

ing is done as follows, breathing through the nose, and paying close attention to each breath:

1. Breath quietly for a few minutes, noticing how you breathe. Relax.
2. Exhale as fully as possible by pulling in your belly at the end of the exhalation, and exhaling a little more air.
3. Now inhale deeply. Your belly, having just been contracted, will naturally expand as you inhale. Visualize the breath being slowly gathered into the abdomen.
4. Continue, exhaling deeply by pulling in your belly, and inhaling deeply by letting your belly expand.

Deep abdominal breathing fully expands and oxygenates the lungs. By letting the belly out on the inhale, the diaphragm is pulled downward so that air rushes all the way into the lungs. This is a full, deep breath, and is quite different from the shallow breathing that most of us do in our every day lives.

Breathing in this manner strengthens the lungs and diaphragm, and allows you to increase the volume of air, and therefore the amount of oxygen, that you take in with each breath. It also relaxes your breathing, and lowers the body's center of gravity, thus reinforcing its stability.

Your breathing should be deep, quiet, and long. *Deep* means that the breath is directed to the lower abdomen so that the lungs can be fully expanded. *Quiet* means that the breath is soft and relaxed, not strained. *Long* means that each breath is done slowly and fully, which increases the duration of each breath.

You will notice that in the Greater Energy exercises, the body movements and the breath patterns flow together. In general, you inhale when the arms are moving either upward, forward, or outward, since these motions naturally expand the ribs. Similarly, you exhale when the arms are moving either downward, backward or inward.

The Flow of the Movements

The Greater Energy exercises should be done with smooth, flowing motions. Many of the exercises involve circular movements of the body. When practiced slowly and gracefully, they gently stretch and loosen the muscles, tendons, and joints. This aids the release and flow of life energy in the meridians.

The eyes usually move with the head. Relax your head, neck, and eyes, and allow them to move together smoothly. These movements also loosen tension in the neck area.

Keep a steady rhythm in your movements. Establish a slow, even tempo that is comfortable for you and maintain it throughout the exercise. This type of slow, steady practice increases the power and effectiveness of each exercise.

Remember always to relax completely after practicing these exercises, so that the *chi* energy released by them can flow and establish a balance in the body.

Body Awareness and Posture

Be conscious of your body and your movements as you practice the exercises. When you are alert and paying attention to what you're doing you get more out of an exercise. Attention is actually *more* important than a physical exertion of strength in order to get the most out of the exercises. It's best to be physically relaxed and mentally alert when practicing. Movement awareness decreases unnecessary exertion, harmonizes the nervous system, and paves the way for meditation.

Always tune into your body during your exercise practice. Close your eyes and focus your attention on how your body feels. "Look" inwardly at different parts of your body and notice the sensations you are experiencing.

Do the exercises without strain, letting your body tell you how far to stretch. Don't worry about limitations; we are all individuals with varying needs and abilities. Remember that your pace will vary from day to day in any case, depending on how you feel, the time of day, the stressful situations you are handling, etc. Trust your judgment. Be flexible and recognize that whatever your level of ability may be, it is right for you; you will improve with regular practice, not with pushing yourself.

The Greater Energy exercises can be practiced at various times during the day, easily fitting into your daily schedule. This is a great advantage, as you don't have to practice them at a regimented time; they can be done spontaneously while watching TV or while talking on the phone, reading, or waiting in line. This makes it much easier to find the time to practice the exercises.

The exercises will also help you increase your awareness of your body at various times throughout the day. This can enable you to recognize poor postural habits so that you can begin to correct them. As your awareness of your body unfolds you will experience a centering, a grounding, a way of taking care of and loving yourself. The more in touch with your body you are, the more you will understand its needs and expressions.

You can cultivate good posture through practicing the Greater Energy exercises and the greater awareness of your body that will result. Good posture comes from a balance of all parts of the body, from your feet to your head.

Classical Chinese exercise manuals say, "The feet act as the roots, motivated by the thighs, controlled by the waist, and manifested in the fingers. From feet to waist there should be unison in movements."

Aim for a coordination of the body as a whole. Note that the stability of the body is based on the stability of the feet, and that the waist is the axis for movement.

Good posture involves an elongation of the spine. To accomplish this, imagine that a straight cord is being pulled directly upward from the top of your head. Also, tilt your pelvis slightly forward to counteract the tendency to extend it backward. Be sure, however, to relax as much as possible while doing this. These instructions should not be cause for forcing any motion or posture.

Check your posture from time to time while practicing your exercises. Make sure that your spine is straight and your body is relaxed. Let your breathing be easy and deep. Enjoy feeling and moving your body.

The position of the following eight parts of the body make up one's posture. All are interrelated. Develop an awareness of each area and discover how it affects the dynamics of the whole body.

1. **Head**: In many of the exercises it is best to draw in the chin toward the chest. This elongates the cervical spine of the neck, allowing the cerebrospinal fluid to circulate freely in the neck and head area. Suspending the head in this way helps nourish the brain, and enables the head and spine to be properly aligned.

2. Shoulders: When the shoulders are relaxed they are loose and comfortable. If they are tight, however, they will be somewhat raised up with the tension. This is a key area since most people have some tension in their shoulders. Uptightness, impatience, or any stress often shows up in shoulder and neck tension.

3. Arms: The arms are related to the shoulders. When the shoulders are tense, they block the *chi* energy from flowing properly to the arms, which can cause tension in the arms, especially the elbow joints. The elbows should be loose and relaxed, moving easily and smoothly.

4. Torso: The trunk of the body has upper and lower parts, divided by the diaphragm. Both the chest and the abdomen should be loose and relaxed. Breathing should be deep, involving the entire torso, not just the chest.

5. Back: With good posture, the spine is elongated so that its natural curves are lessened. These two curves are located in the neck and lower back areas. With poor posture they are accentuated, with a slump in the upper back, and a backward tilt to the pelvis in the lower back (protrusion of the buttocks).

When the spine is straight and elongated, the head, neck, back and pelvis are aligned. This helps keep the spine loose and flexible, and keeps the body in balance.

6. Waist: The upper and lower parts of the body should move in coordination; the waist is the link between them. Relaxing the waist allows the *chi* energy to flow freely between the upper and lower torso.

Tension in the waist can put a strain on the muscles of the whole torso. But if the waist is loose and free, the *chi* is able to flow through the meridians which run up and down the body.

7. Pelvis: The pelvis is the base for the spine. If thrown out of alignment, it affects the entire spine and thus the entire torso. Let your pelvis be relaxed and tilted slightly forward.

8. Legs: The movement of the legs gives the body strength, stability, and helps to coordinate the body's equilibrium.

Discipline

Discipline is most important when you first begin practicing the Greater Energy exercises. You may feel stiff and may not be able to stretch very far. You may have difficulty in guiding your breathing and in focusing your attention. At this stage, self-discipline will help you keep going.

After you've been practicing the exercises for a while, however, you will probably find that you won't need as much discipline to do them because they're so enjoyable and because you will begin to notice results. Just as you manage to do other things you enjoy without having to make a big effort, you will find the time and opportunity to practice your Greater Energy exercises. Health, like any goal, must be earned by practice. Constant daily practice is the way to success. After one month of doing these exercises every day (at the same time each day, if possible), they will become a natural part of your daily routine, something you'd miss if you didn't do them. The results you will experience will motivate you to continue.

Good health is possible for everyone. Practice these easy exercises and enjoy the good health that Greater Energy brings.

IV

The Greater Energy
Wake-up Routine

Beginning the Day
With Greater Energy

These techniques, simple yet highly beneficial, can be done on a carpet or while lying on your bed.

Wind Shield Wipers

1. Lie on your back comfortably.
2. With your heels remaining on the ground, turn your feet in and out, making a semi-circle with your toes.
3. Breathe deeper than you normally breathe, continuing to turn your toes in and out.
4. Repeat until your legs feel stimulated. It may take several minutes to feel this sensation, but continue seven more times after your leg muscles start to ache.
5. Lie still for a few minutes with your eyes closed to experience the benefits.

Benefits: Cold feet, weak legs, urinary problems, abdominal pain or weakness.

Lazy Marching

1. Lie on your back with your hands resting at your sides, palms facing down.
2. Inhale as you lift up and bend one of your legs.
3. Exhale and relax the leg down.
4. Alternate legs 14 times. This is truly a lazy person's exercise because you don't need to lift a finger.

Benefits: This exercise can strengthen the body with consistent daily practice. Marching on your back benefits the intestinal tract. It has been used to strengthen the urinary-reproductive system, the lower back, and abdominal region. Try it for expelling gas and relieving constipation.

Butterfly

1. Lie on your back with your legs bent, feet flat on the ground.
2. Exhale, gently dropping your knees out to the sides toward the ground.
3. Inhale as your legs come back up.
4. Continue the exercise for about two minutes.

Benefits: The Butterfly is excellent for the reproductive system, swelling in the legs and ankles, lower back problems, pains inside the groin, and excess fear or anger.

Easy Rolls

1. Lie on your back with your legs bent, feet flat on the ground.
2. Fold your arms across your chest and roll from side to side, allowing both of your knees to fall with the rest of the body.

Benefits: This easy exercise massages the entire back, hips and shoulder blades. Pressure on the acupressure points in these areas benefits hypertension, breathing difficulties, nervous disorders, insomnia, bursitis, high blood pressure, back tensions, and overall body pains.

Hip Rolls

1. Lie on your back with your legs bent, feet flat on the ground.
2. Let your knees fall to the right as you turn your head to the left.
3. Continue, reversing sides.
4. Close your eyes and feel the beneficial pressures being applied to your buttock muscles and stretching your lower back.

Benefits: Hip rolls are good for frustration, impatience, hypertension, insomnia, hip pains, sciatica, lower back stiffness, and urinary problems.

Lazy Dance Step

1. Lie on your back with your legs extended straight in line with the rest of your body.
2. Inhale and lift your right leg over your left foot.
3. Lower the heel of the right leg to the left side of the stationary foot. The heel should easily bounce up and over the stationary foot to its original position as you exhale.
4. Repeat the "dance step," alternating your feet, for one minute.

Benefits: This exercise strengthens the abdominal muscles, and stimulates the reflexology points which correspond to the anus, the sciatic nerve, and the brain.

Breathing and Stretching

1. Comfortably breathe slowly and deeply through your nostrils.
2. After several long deep breaths, gently stretch your arms and legs.
3. Let your whole body move and stretch in whatever ways make you feel good, enabling your body to greet the day.
4. Continue to breathe deeply as you slowly rise to a standing position.

Rolling the Head

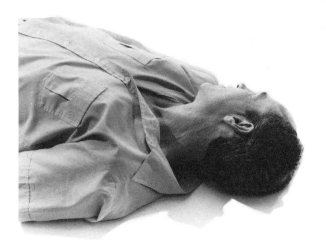

1. Lie on your back with your arms and legs comfortably relaxed.
2. Let your head slowly roll from side to side. Close your eyes and feel your neck relax as your head gently moves.
3. Let your breath be long and deep.
4. Continue the subtle movement until you can completely relax your neck.
5. Finish with your head straight in line with the spinal column.

Benefits: Rolling the head benefits repressed anger, nervous disabilities, insomnia, headaches, pain in general, and depression.

STANDING ROTATIONS

The following movements stretch, lubricate, and strengthen the major joints, tendons, and ligaments for achieving radiant health and longevity.

Looking Around

1. Draw a circle in front of your face with your index finger.
2. Follow the tip of the finger with your eyes.
3. Let your head fall forward, then back, back and forth several times; then side to side.
4. Then follow this by slowly rotating your head around first in one direction and then the other to relax your neck.

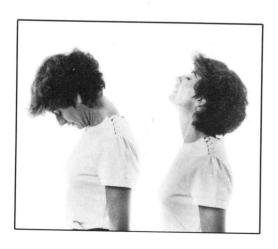

Shoulder Rotations

1. Rotate your shoulders around in one direction and then in the other.

Arm Rotations

1. Swing the arms; one at a time in a large circle.
2. Extend your arms out to the side parallel to the ground, and rotate them in a clockwise then counter-clockwise motion. Start with small circles and finish with larger circles that rotate the whole shoulder socket.

Elbow Rotation

1. Place your hands on your shoulders.
2. Draw seven circles in one direction, then seven circles in the other direction with your elbows.
3. Then inhale forward and exhale to each side seven times.

Waist and Pelvic Rotations

1. Place your hands on your hips with your feet together.
2. Keep your vision on the horizon.
3. Slowly rotate your torso in one direction, and then in the other direction.
4. Continue to rotate your hips with the feet spread one foot apart.
5. Keep your fingers on the sacrum points as illustrated.

Circling the Ball Above the Head

1. Place your hands over your head.
2. Make a circular motion with your hands as if you are holding a large colorful beach ball.

Knee Rotations

1. Place your hands on your knees.
2. Bend down as you make a circular motion with your knees.
3. Repeat seven times for each direction.

Whole Body Rotation: Turning the Heaven and Earth

1. Bring both your hands up, above your head, making the same circular motion as in the Circling Ball exercise.
2. Begin with a small circle, increasing the size of the sphere. Then, gradually expand the size of the circle even more by encompassing the space in front of you.
3. The rotation of both arms gracefully changes from a horizontal circle above your head to a large verticle circle in front of your body.*
4. Your breath should deepen naturally on its own after a full minute of practice. Continue the movement with the breath, inhaling as your hands circulate upward and exhaling as they come toward the ground.

---

*If you begin to feel dizzy, immediately change the direction of your arms. This will counterbalance your equilibrium. Continue for about three minutes until changing directions loses its effectiveness. Whenever possible, finish by lying down comfortably on your back with your eyes closed and relax for at least ten minutes.

V

Ten Minutes
to Greater Energy

LYING DOWN EXERCISES:
A TEN-MINUTE SERIES

Leg Hugs

1. Lie on your back with your arms resting at your sides. Allow your body to relax as you consciously breathe deeply.
2. After a minute, inhale, bringing your left leg up toward your chest with your knee bent.
3. Clasp both of your hands around the left knee and draw it into your chest, using your arm muscles.
4. Use the heels of your hands to press both sides of the leg, just below the knee. This stimulates several vital acupressure points.
5. Hold this position while taking three long, deep breaths.
6. Unclasp your hands as you begin the fourth inhalation, allowing your left leg to straighten and lower to the floor.
7. Repeat this exercise with your right leg.
8. Continue alternating legs in this way for approximately three minutes.

Benefits: This exercise releases tension in the abdominal area, groin and pelvis. The yogis call this exercise "Wind Relieving Pose" because the position helps to release gas. It can prevent flatulence when practiced for several weeks along with proper dietary considerations.

The acupressure points pressed in this posture benefit the gastro-intestinal system. A person with constipation, indigestion, or lower back pain would benefit enormously by practicing this exercise twice a day for three weeks.

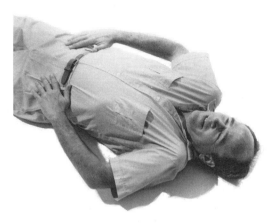

Shoulder Rotations

1. Raise and lower your shoulders until the movement stimulates your respiration.
2. Place your hands on your thighs. Rotate your shoulders in a complete circle seven times in each direction.

Benefits: This exercise releases tension in the shoulders and relieves fatigue.

Dragon Turning the Sea

1. Move your tongue around your mouth in between your lips and your front teeth. This will stimulate the secretion of saliva.
2. When your mouth is full of saliva, swallow the liquid in three parts.

Benefits: The secretion of saliva aids to balance the digestive system and enables internal organs to detoxify the body.

Genital Rejuvenation

A. Polishing the Organs of Origin

This exercise should be done in privacy.
1. Rub the abdomen in a circular motion 81 times as your other hand holds your genital organs.
2. Women should cup their palm over their vagina. This prevents menstrual cramps, pain, and relieves abdominal stress, especially during pregnancy.
3. Men should hold their penis and scrotum with one hand as the other hand moves around the abdomen. This exercise can enable a man to gain control of the release of his sperm by improving the efficiency of the reproductive and digestive organs.

B. Raising the Rectum

This is an internal exercise that cannot be seen externally.
1. Powerfully contract the rectum, sex organs, and the muscles of the abdomen.
2. Hold this contraction for several seconds before relaxing.

Benefits: The internal organs of the lower abdomen, especially the intestines and sexual organs, benefit when you pull your abdomen inward. This, along with the contraction of the rectum, stimulates several acupressure points around the sacrum, which further strengthens the sexual organs. Raising the rectum also helps to prevent hemorrhoids and constipation.

Leg Rotations

This exercise should be done in moderation.

1. Raise one leg at a time, drawing a circle the size of a large beach ball with your toes pointed forward.
2. First practice the rotation of the leg from outside to inside, and then reverse the direction.
3. Finish by drawing a circle with both legs.

An advanced practitioner can practice drawing a circle three feet in diameter with both legs held together. Circulate the feet in one direction several times and then change the direction.

Benefits: This exercise strengthens the intestines and releases intestinal gas.

Draw a Cross with Both Legs

1. Inhale, raising up both legs a foot off the ground.
2. While they are in the air, spread the legs apart.
3. Bring them back together, raising the legs straight up to a 45 degree angle from the floor.
4. Exhale, lowering the legs back down to the floor.

Benefits: This exercise strengthens the abdominal muscles and tonifies the body as a whole. Deep relaxation should immediately follow the exercise, with your eyes closed.

Heel Massage

1. Lie on your back. Use your heels to massage the four acupressure points illustrated.
2. Rub your heel back and forth over a 3 to 4 inch area, stimulating each of these vital points 49 times on both sides of your body.

You will feel a sensation of pain at the point which will "hurt good." In other words, the pain will actually feel beneficial if you are doing the heel massage properly. Totally relax on your back with your eyes closed after rubbing the following four acupressure points with your heel.

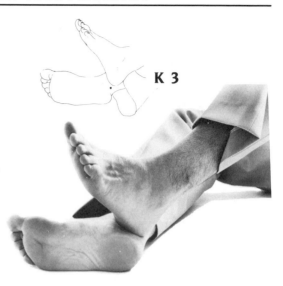

Kidney 1 "Bubbling Spring"

Traditional Associations: Hypertension, body painful and stiff, difficulty sleeping, loss of appetite, chest and ribs feel full, constipation, retention of urine, head congestion.

Kidney 3 "Flowing Stream"

Traditional Associations: Impotence, oversleeping, cold legs and feet, heels swollen and painful, lower backaches, hands stiff or frozen, urine dark yellow, defecation difficult.

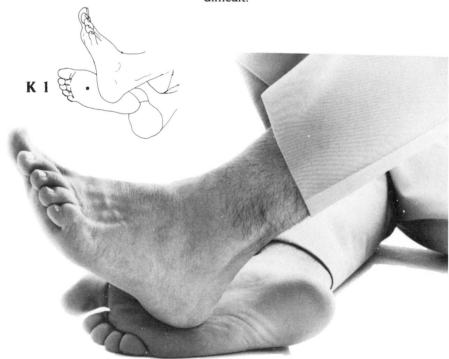

Stomach 36 "Three Miles"

Traditional Associations: Fatigue, abdominal swelling or pain, gastritis, intestinal noises, indigestion, constipation, legs weak, lack of energy.

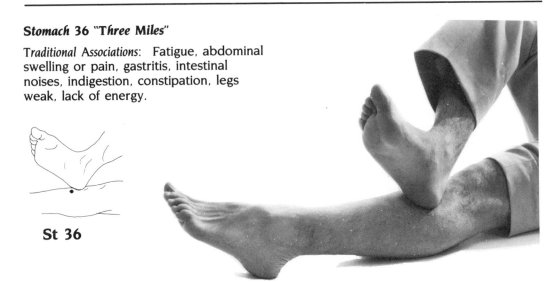

St 36

Gall Bladder 40 "Molehill"

Traditional Associations: Impatience, difficulty in breathing, pain in buttocks, muscular spasms, sciatica, sides of body ache, neck swollen or painful.

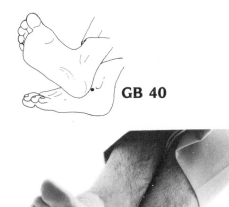

GB 40

Guidance for Deep Relaxation

After doing a set of exercises, remain on your back, palms facing up. Close your eyes and feel your body relaxing. Wiggle your toes, letting them relax. Rotate your feet so that the ankles relax. Slightly move your legs, feeling your calves, knees and thighs relax.

Tighten your buttocks muscles and let them relax. Feel your sex organs and pelvis relax. Take several breaths into your abdominal area, letting your belly relax. Just let yourself relax. Whatever you are hanging onto inside your mind, just let it go....

Let your whole back relax. Relax your arms. Feel each finger relax. Tell your shoulders and neck to relax. Let go of any tension in your forehead and eyebrows. Let your temples and ears relax. Lips, teeth, and tongue...relax. Move your jaw from side to side, letting it relax. Relax your nose and throat and tell your eyes to relax. Feel your whole body totally loose and relaxed, and experience the benefits....

SITTING STRETCHES:
A FIVE-MINUTE SERIES

by Dani Riggs

WE HAVE BECOME a sitting culture. Most of us have jobs that require us to spend large parts of our day sitting at a desk or in front of a computer display terminal. Our waiting rooms, theaters, restaurants and transportation systems have us sitting in chairs. A frequent complaint is "How am I going to exercise if I have to sit here all day?" At home we can be seen sitting reading or in front of a TV or another computer display terminal.

The lack of movement leads to stagnation in our muscles, joints and internal organs. Back problems, a leading cause of lost work days, are caused or worsened by sitting in poor postures and from a lack of movement. Constipation and digestive problems are also leading causes of pain, discomfort and eventually serious illness. But these problems can be eliminated. In order to stay loose, limber, healthy and youthful, our bodies need movement.

Since many of us have to spend most of our time sitting, the following stretch exercises are designed for that position. In fact, most of these can only be done while sitting comfortably in a chair. The steps of each exercise are outlined and some of the specific benefits for each stretch are listed. Even though you may be working on one of the specific problems listed under a particular stretch, it is recommended that you complete all six stretches on a regular daily basis for best results. Using specific stretches, as indicated, for different stressful situations can also be helpful. An example would be to use the kidney stretch for a fearful situation. It is recommended that each stretch be repeated three to five times. Remember, you can use these stretch exercises whether you are at the office, on a bench, at home or at school. If possible, after completing these exercises, meditate or relax with your eyes closed for at least a few mintues to fully discover the benefits.

Holding the Sky
With Two Hands

1. Sit comfortably in a chair with your back straight and legs shoulder-width apart.
2. Start with your hands and arms hanging loosely at your sides. Inhale, raising both hands over your head and turn the palms up toward the ceiling.
3. Look up at your hands allowing your head to tilt back.
4. Press your palms toward the ceiling.
5. Exhale, letting your hands come down by your sides.
6. Repeat the exercise four more times.

Benefits: This exercise is good for the lungs and large intestine. Problems with constipation and congestion can be helped. It is also helpful for problems associated with the nose. The emotions of grief and anxiety can be lessened by doing this stretch. This chair exercise is also excellent for relieving tension in the shoulders.

Right Hand Stretch

1. Start with your hands hanging loosely at your sides.
2. Inhale, raising both hands over your head; interlace your fingers and turn your palms upward. Press upward with both palms.
3. Press harder with the right palm, and exhale. This will put a greater stretch on the right side.
4. Let your hands move slowly back to your side and repeat the exercise.

Benefits: This exercise is good for the liver and gall bladder. Menstrual problems, eye problems and difficulties digesting fats can be helped through this exercise. It is excellent for dealing with excessive or repressed anger. The next time someone or some situation really angers you, try this stretch and see how it affects your mood. It is also a good stretch to do before you sit down and try to plan a trip or project.

Left Hand Stretch

This stretch is identical to the liver stretch except that when you press upward with the palms, you press harder with the left side.

Benefits: The heart and small intestine are benefitted by this stretch. It is good for chest pains, insomnia and arm pain. It can be used to help lessen feelings of sadness or anxiety. It is helpful in situations where you need to see things clearly.

Scooping the Ribs

1. Bend forward slightly at the waist and look up toward the ceiling at a 45 degree angle.
2. Place your fingertips just below your left rib cage. This corresponds with the location of the stomach, spleen and pancreas. Inhale deeply.
3. Exhale and slowly press into this point.
4. Repeat the exercise, using full deep breaths and exhaling completely.

Benefits: This stretch is good for the spleen, pancreas and stomach. These are the organs responsible for nourishing the body, cultivating greater energy and a feeling of security. It is helpful for menstrual cramps, constipation, edema, abdominal disorders and fatigue. This stretch can also be helpful in dealing with stress, worry and depression.

Arms Around the Knees

1. Bring your legs and feet together.
2. Interlace your fingers and place them around your knees.
3. Look up toward the ceiling at a 45 degree angle.
4. Inhale deeply and straighten your back.
5. Exhale, pulling in the stomach, flexing the back and pulling on your arms.

Benefits: This stretch is good for the kidneys and bladder. It is helpful with problems such as back trouble, hemorrhoids, sciatica, retention of urine, stiff neck, menstrual disorders and dysfunctions of sexual organs.

Ragdoll in a Chair

1. Return to sitting with your feet shoulder-width apart.
2. Raise your right foot up and, bending the knee, place your right ankle bone in the hollow just above your left knee cap.
3. Inhale deeply and exhale, lowering your body over your left thigh, letting your left arm fall over your left side and your right arm fall just to the right of your left knee.
4. Staying in this position, inhale deeply and exhale three times.
5. Then inhale and rise up to sitting position.
6. Switch sides so that your left ankle bone is above your right knee and repeat the exercise.

Benefits: This exercise is good for all of the internal organs. You should feel a good stretch in the pelvis, along the insides of the thighs and along the back. It is particularly good for lower back problems.

EASY SELF-MASSAGE:
A FIVE-MINUTE SERIES

Beating the Heavenly Drum

This exercise knocks on the base of the skull.

1. Sitting comfortably, place your middle fingers on the occipital bone at the base of your skull, and cross the index fingers over the middle fingers.
2. Cover your ears firmly with the palms of your hands.
3. Snap the index fingers against the middle fingers, onto the occipital ridge for approximately one minute. Listen to this drum-like sound in your inner ear.

Benefits: Beating the Heavenly Drum activates a key acupressure point called "wind pond," which regulates brain activity. It is related to the eyes and also benefits one's equilibrium.

Listening to the Heavenly Thunder

1. Seal your ears again with the palms of your hands, as in "Beating the Heavenly Drum," but let your fingers simply rest on the base of your skull.
2. Close your eyes and knock your back molars together.

Benefits: The Heavenly Thunder awakens your brain and activates your mental powers.

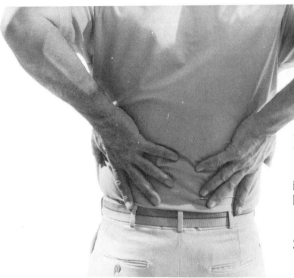

Rubbing the Eyes of the Kidney

Evidence from the ancient Chinese internal health arts indicates that you can help kidney imbalances yourself.
1. Rub your lower back with the palms of your hands, creating warmth.
2. Breathe deeply into the heat in the lower back for a few minutes and feel the energy recharging the kidneys.

Benefits: Releases lower back stiffness and pain. Daily practice is good for the kidneys and the reproductive system.

Rubbing the Hands

1. Rub your hands together rapidly, producing electricity and warmth.
2. Quickly cup your hands over your eyes and rotate the heels of your hands over your eyes, absorbing the warmth.

Benefits: The energy produced in Rubbing the Hands benefits circulation and provides healing heat for the eyes.

Changing Grip

1. Sitting comfortably, bring your hands behind your back. Have the palm of one hand facing you and the palm of the other facing away from you. Link your hands together by keeping your fingers curved so that they are interlocked.
2. Pull your hands apart, creating a firm pressure for a couple of seconds with the two opposing forces.
3. Switch the position of your hands by rotating your wrists, and pull them apart again.
4. Continue the changing grips five more times.

Benefits: This easy exercise has been traditionally used for reducing hypertension and preventing insomnia.

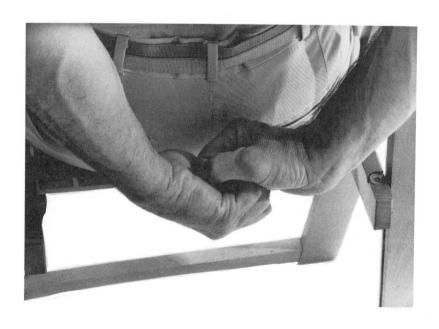

Dry Wash

A. Facial Massage

1. Rub your hands together, creating a heat.
2. Immediately afterwards thoroughly massage your face and neck.

Benefits: A daily dry wash cleans the pores, restoring tone and luster to the skin. This makes the face look younger and more attractive.*

B. Eye Massage

1. Use the heels of your hands in a circular motion to gently massage the eyeballs, lids and bony ridges around your eyes.
2. The back of the thumbs can also be used to circulate around these ridges.

Benefits: This exercise benefits the liver, digestion, eyestrain, vision problems and nervous conditions.

---

*You can also vigorously massage the rest of your body in the privacy of your home. It should be done strongly and quickly, taking 5 to 10 minutes. This self-massage is most effective naked but can be done over clothes.

C. *Pressure Beside the Nose*

1. Use the tips of your middle fingers to massage up and down from the base of the nose between the eyes to the sides of the nostrils several times.

Benefits: This exercise benefits sinusitis, colds, influenza and constipation.

D. *The Jaws and Temples*

1. With the heels of your hands, rub up and down the sides of your face from your jaws to your temples about 36 times.
2. Massage this area in a circular motion with your fingertips, using firm pressure on the jaw muscles. The temples also benefit from a gentle circular motion which pulls the skin in all directions.

Benefits: This exercise is good for headaches, the brain and nervous system, and it also can improve vision.

The Ears

A. Plug the Ears

1. Place your middle fingers into the opening of the ears.
2. Plug and unplug the ears by moving your fingers in and out about 28 times.

Benefits: This can help prevent ear inflammations and infections.

B. Drilling the Auditory Canal

1. Place the tip of your middle fingers gently into the ears.
2. Close your eyes and rotate your hand back and forth for 30 seconds, massaging the opening of the auditory canal.

Benefits: This exercise is beneficial for hearing.

C. Palming the Ears

1. Press on your ears with your palms and then let go creating pressure and suction.
2. Repeat seven times. A noise is made as you move your palms away.

Benefits: This exercise benefits the inner ear and activates the brain.

Stretching the Neck

1. Interlace your fingers together behind your neck.
2. Inhale as you tilt your head back, and stretch your elbows up and backward.
3. Exhale, letting your head and elbows slowly relax forward.
4. Continue to inhale up and exhale down, completing 14 cycles.

Benefits: This exercise prevents stiff necks, tightness in the shoulders and helps to improve general circulation.

Meditate or relax on your back with your eyes closed for at least a few minutes to assimilate the benefits of these exercises.

STANDING EXERCISES:
A TEN-MINUTE SERIES

Upholding Heaven With The Two Hands

1. Stand with your feet comfortably apart and your arms at your sides. Keep your eyes open during this exercise.
2. Inhale, raising your arms out to the sides and up above your head.
3. With your palms facing down, interlock your fingers. Rotate your hands so that your palms face the sky. Look up at the back of your hands. Inhale more, stretching upward as if you are upholding heaven.
4. Exhale and let your arms float down to your sides.
5. Repeat 5 or 6 times.

Benefits: This longevity exercise strengthens the body as a whole. It harmonizes the three major segments or "warmers" of the trunk. The upper segment controls the respiratory system, the middle houses the digestive system, and the lower segment governs the excretory and sexual functions. Upholding Heaven With the Two Hands stretches the Triple Warmer Meridian which harmonizes the vital organs in each of these segments. According to the classical teachings of the Chinese sages, this exercise unifies the relationships between the internal organs, improves circulation and releases shoulder tension. The stretch also benefits the muscular system and helps prevent arthritis. The tendons and ligaments are stretched, increasing the circulation to the extremities.

Opening the Bow

1. Stand with your feet comfortably apart.
2. Cross your arms in front of you at the level of your heart and clench your fists firmly. Imagine you are holding a large bow.
3. Turn your head to the left, the direction you are going to visualize shooting the arrow. Use your imagination to aim very far, as if shooting the arrow toward an eagle.
4. Inhale deeply as you open the bow, and bring your left arm straight to the left as if pulling the bow forward. Simultaneously, bend your right arm and pull your fist toward your right shoulder, as if pulling the bow string back.
5. Exhale as you gently release the bow, crossing your arms in front of your chest once again.
6. Repeat the exercise on the right side.
7. Practice the exercise three times on each side, breathing with the movement.

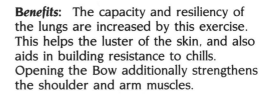

Benefits: The capacity and resiliency of the lungs are increased by this exercise. This helps the luster of the skin, and also aids in building resistance to chills. Opening the Bow additionally strengthens the shoulder and arm muscles.

Raising the Arms One At a Time

1. Stand with your feet comfortably apart and your arms crossed in front of your solar plexus.
2. Inhale and raise your left hand straight above your head with the palm facing the sky, the fingers turned inward. The right hand is simultaneously lowered to the thigh with your right palm facing the ground, fingers turned inward. Bring your head back during the exhalation.
3. Exhale and return your arms and head to starting position.
4. Repeat the movement on the other side, raising your right arm while lowering your left.
5. Alternate sides, practicing the movement six times in all.

Benefits: The spleen and stomach are adjusted and harmonized through the movement of this exercise. The Large and Small Intestine Meridians, which run along the arms, are also regulated from this stretch. The balancing points for the Triple Warmer Meridian at the back of the wrists are stimulated to further aid in balancing the digestive system.

Looking Behind

1. Stand with your arms crossed in front of your upper chest. Keep the chin tucked into the hollow of the throat, stretching the back of the neck.
2. Inhale deeply, open your arms to a 45 degree angle from the sides of your body, and turn your head toward the left, looking as far behind you as possible. Pull your arms back, arching the chest up and out. You will feel the stretch in your arms, wrists, neck and also in your eyes as you look behind.
3. Exhale, returning your head and arms forward.
4. Repeat the same movement, turning to the right side. Alternate sides, practicing the movement six times in all.

Benefits: Looking Behind rejuvenates the five yin (nourishing) organs, the heart, spleen, lungs, kidney and liver. The movement also naturally expands the capacity of the lungs. If practiced twice daily, this simple breathing exercise can help prevent stiff necks. In this exercise, several internal points in the shoulder and upper back areas are pressed, strengthening general resistance. Therefore, the Chinese say "Look behind and leave the five diseases and seven injuries."

69

Swaying the Head and Wagging the Tail

1. Stand with the legs spread apart. Bend your knees into a "horse riding" position, with your feet flat on the ground, your knees directly above your toes and your weight balanced.
2. Place your hands above the knees with your fingers on the inside and your thumbs rotated outwards.
3. Inhale and arch your spine, bringing your head back and your chest up and out.

4. Exhale down, bending forward so that you are looking between your legs.
5. Inhale, returning to the starting position, with your spine straight. Exhale and bend your whole torso to the left side, keeping your spine, neck and head in a straight line.
6. Inhale up to the starting position again. Exhale and bend to the right side, tilting your shoulders and head to the right.
7. Repeat steps 3 through 6 twice more.
8. Rotate the hips and trunk of the body, several times in one direction and then in the other direction.
9. Rotate the head slowly clockwise and then counter-clockwise.

VARIATION:

Swaying the Head

1. Stand with the legs spread apart. Bend your knees into a "horse riding" position, with your feet flat on the ground, your knees directly above your toes and your weight balanced.
2. Join your hands by interlocking your thumbs, palms facing out.
3. Stretch your arms straight up toward the sky.
4. Keeping your arms straight, draw a large clockwise circle with your hands so that the fingers almost touch the floor as your hands go around.
5. As you come up to center, do the same circle in a counter-clockwise direction. Sometimes people get dizzy when practicing this exercise. This can be alleviated by moving more slowly, and by being sure to always change the direction and turn the opposite way around to balance and restore the equilibrium.

Benefits: This exercise strengthens and balances the digestive organs, the lower back and helps to reduce fat around the hips and waist. The ancients in China also practiced this exercise to improve the circulation and condition of the heart. This exercise eliminates the excess "fire" (tension) that tends to accumulate in the heart. Too much "fire" in the heart can lead to headaches, hypertension, excessive anger and frustration. According to the Chinese, most high blood pressure patients can help themselves tremendously by avoiding red meat, salt and by practicing this exercise three times daily.

71

Clenching the Fists With Attentive Eyes

1. Stand with the feet apart and the knees bent slightly.
2. Make a fist with your palms facing up by your waist.
3. Inhale, open your eyes wide, firmly clench your molars together and smile.
4. Slowly exhale as you firmly punch your fist diagonally in front, turning the fist over so it faces downward when fully extended.
5. Inhale as you slowly clench the arm inward back to the waist.
6. Repeat the exercise on the other side, alternating four times.

Benefits: This exercise releases tensions in the arms and the chest. It strengthens the vital organs and especially benefits the liver.

Stretching Backward

1. Place your palms over your lower back with your fingers positioned downward.
2. Inhale, arching your back with your eyes also looking backward. Bend your knees in this position to increase the bend.
3. Gently bend backward 7 times, as you exhale.
4. Inhale up to an erect standing position.
5. Exhale as you gently drop your head and upper portion of your body forward. Grasp hold of all of your toes. Allow your neck to relax in this position.
6. Slowly return to a standing position as you inhale. Repeat the exercise 7 times.

Benefits: This exercise further rejuvenates all of the internal organs, especially the kidneys. Ancient sages claim that it will eliminate 100 diseases.

Pulling on the Legs

1. Standing comfortably, inhale and stretch your arms forward and up, stretching up high.
2. Exhale down and grasp your calf muscles. Use your arm muscles to pull your heels up off the ground for a couple of seconds.
3. Spring up on to the balls of your feet six times.
4. Now place the palms of your hands over your knee caps and rub them in a circular motion.

Benefits: This exercise benefits the kidneys, the lower back and the sciatic nerve. It also helps to prevent leg cramps.

Swing Hands

This is an ancient exercise that has been handed down from generation to generation. *Swing Hands* enables the body to accumulate vital energy through the breath. It improves circulation which energizes, awakens, and balances the body's energy, contributing to a person's experience of health and well-being.

The Chinese have documented numerous cases demonstrating that *Swing Hands* can aid conditions such as insomnia, poor appetite, high blood pressure and heart trouble, eye problems, hemorrhoids, neurasthenia, and problems related to the liver, stomach, kidneys, and other internal organs.

Many of us live sedentary lives; we don't use our bodies enough to keep them vibrant and healthy. When you sit a lot, for example, the movement of the lungs is restricted, the digestive organs are compressed, and their proper functioning is thus hampered. Also, circulation is not stimulated the way it is by active movement, and can become sluggish. Many health problems are either caused or worsened by an insufficient air supply and poor circulation.

The practice of *Swing Hands* can reverse our sedentary tendency. It is the simplest possible exercise besides walking, yet it moves and stretches the body, deepens the breathing, and improves circulation.

Directions:

1. Stand erect with your feet parallel and shoulder-width apart.
2. Grasp the earth with your toes by firmly curling them. If you wear shoes, your toes will grip the soles of the shoes.
3. Tighten your buttock muscles and contract your anus. This raises the rectum, which strengthens the reproductive and eliminatory systems. If you later notice that you've forgotten and have stopped doing the contraction, simply resume it.
4. Relax your upper body, including your chest, back, shoulders, arms, neck, head, face, and jaw.
5. Let your eyes look straight ahead, or close them if you prefer.
6. Swing your hands back and forth. As your arms come forward, they are parallel to the ground with the palms facing down. Vigorously swing them back to the limit of the arms' range of motion. This force leads directly to the easy forward swing, as action leads to reaction.

Count how many times you swing your hands. Start slowly, with one hundred swings. You can gradually build this up to two, four, five hundred, or even one thousand swings. For the greatest benefit, practice whenever you can, at various times during the day.

The feeling to cultivate is that of the upper body light and relaxed, and the lower portion of the body fully grounded and substantial. Let the back be straight and easy, with the head straight, as if being pulled up by a string. This will elongate the neck.

The shoulders, arms, hands, wrists, and elbows should be loose, moving easily. The chest should feel relaxed and open, allowing the breath to deepen naturally with the movement. The head, face, and jaw should be calm and relaxed.

As you practice, be aware of your body, your breath, your motion. Feel the aliveness, and enjoy it!

VI

Breathing Techniques

BREATHING TECHNIQUES

THE BREATH IS the most profound tool known for purifying and revitalizing the body. Something as basic as the breath reflects how you feel about yourself, as well as how you relate to the world. If your breath is shallow, all of your body's vital systems will be functioning at a minimum level. If your breath is long and deep, however, the respiratory system can function fully and properly, and oxygenation of the body cells will be complete.

There is a close correlation between the physiology of the breath and the psychology of behavior, since the way you feel physically affects your vitality, how you feel emotionally, and how you interact in the world. Because breathing is a key to physical well-being, or to the lack of it, it has a large part to play in determining how we feel emotionally from day to day.

According to traditional Chinese physiology, the human potential lies within the kidneys, the body's energy storage tanks. The Chinese invented deep breathing exercises to charge these organs with vital energy. Deep breathing increases both the amount of fully oxygenated red blood cells, and the release of the waste product,

carbon dioxide, which chemically changes into carbonic acid if not eliminated through proper respiration. Accumulated carbonic acid must be filtered by the kidneys, and this taxes your body's essential energy. The following are five breathing techniques important to practice for obtaining greater energy.

Long Deep Breathing is the most basic technique for balancing the meridian pathways, the endocrine system, and the emotions. Inhale deeply into the abdomen, the diaphragm, and finally into the chest. Hold the breath for a few seconds, then exhale slowly. Consciously breathe smoothly, gradually, and deeply, concentrating on making each breath full and complete.

Hara Breathing nourishes the internal organs, giving the body power and endurance. The Hara is a vital energy center located three finger-widths below the navel, at the acupressure point Conception Vessel 6. Concentrate on this point while breathing deeply into the lower abdomen. Let your belly come out as you inhale. Feel the breath being expanded into the depths of the belly. Exhale, drawing the belly in, letting the energy circulate throughout the body. Directing the breath through the "Sea of Energy," as the Hara is called, strengthens the general condition of the body.

Breath Visualizations tap the infinite creativity of the mind by focusing on certain parts of the body. With the breath, the potential for self-directed actualization and healing expands. Breath visualizations use the power of the imagination to unblock areas of the body, promoting new awareness, positive attitudes, and a greater circulation of energy. There are endless variations and possibilities for visualizations, the one chosen being determined by the individual's condition, and the particular situation that the person wishes to affect. Different combinations of color, sound, body parts, guided meditations, and physical, mental, and emotional affirmations help to channel the power of the breath. The following is an example of a simple visualization that helps "breathe away your tension" and replaces it with vital energy.

Close your eyes, and focus on an area of your body that needs attention. Imagine that the breath is a substance that is penetrating into that area. Concentrate on breathing into the blockage. If the tension is in your neck, for example, breathe deeply into all those tight muscles. Hold the breath a couple of seconds at the top of the inhalation. Exhale, smoothly allowing your tension to let go. Use the breath as a tool for releasing stress. Again, inhale deeply, concentrating on bringing your breath into the affected area. Exhale, feeling this energy circulate throughout your entire body.

Breath of Fire is a powerful Yogic technique used with the postures. It strengthens the nervous system, cleanses the blood, and expands the body's capacity to assimilate energy. The Breath of Fire consists of short, rapid breathing through the nose (making about one breath per second), concentrating on pumping the breath out by contracting the abdomen. This technique also stimulates the nerves in the nasal passages, and charges the body with immediate energy.

Holding a Deep Breath serves to massage different internal parts of the body. The depth of the breath along with this internal massage heightens the body's ability to develop a greater capacity to produce and utilize human electrical energy.

COORDINATING ENERGY AND MOVEMENT
by Dani Riggs

THE ABILITY TO gain greater energy can be developed by using your body correctly. This can be achieved by coordinating simple movements with slow, deep breathing. The exercises in this section focus on gentle, easy movements to use with breath control for increasing your vitality.

In our culture we think of exercises as being hard or difficult. Many expect that at the end of a workout we should be sweaty and worn out. Some exercise programs can leave us feeling weak and sore. This creates more aching muscles and tight tendons instead of getting rid of them, resulting in a stiff, hard body.

The following energy exercise movements gently coordinate all parts of the body. They are effective for getting rid of sore and stiff places by relieving tensions. Their emphasis is on relaxation. At the end of a workout you will feel energized, refreshed and clear-headed. The goal is to create a body with a smooth, even energy flow bringing health and vitality.

Standing Exercise Instructions: Once you have learned these exercises, it should take ten to fifteen minutes to do the whole set.

Belly Breathing

1. Stand with feet parallel and shoulder-width apart.
2. Relax and slightly bend your ankles, knees and lower back. In this position, the bottom of your pelvis should be tipped slightly forward.
3. Relax your shoulders and arms. Look straight ahead with your head level.
4. Breathe deeply and fully into your abdomen, below your navel. As you inhale, allow your belly to swell; as you exhale, draw your stomach in. Let your breathing be full, relaxed and natural.
5. Stand like this for 10 to 20 breathing cycles.

Easy Rider

1. Continue the procedure in Belly Breathing, but as you inhale, bend your knees, slightly lowering your body.
2. Exhale, rising back up to your original position. Remember not to strain, so bend your knees just a little.
3. Repeat this exercise seven times at first. With practice you can do more repetitions (10 to 20 times) and allow yourself to bend your knees further.

Arm Circles

1. Continue the procedure in Easy Rider and then raise your arms to shoulder height.
2. Allow your arms to curve in gently, bending at the elbow and wrist. Your arms are facing your chest.
3. As you bend your knees and inhale, your hands should curve toward your body.

4. As you straighten your legs and exhale, your hands open away from your body and return to their original position in front of your chest.
5. Move slowly and fluidly, repeating this exercise seven times. Remember to keep breathing and stay relaxed.

Palms In—Pushing Out

1. Combine the hand positions from Arm Circles and Palm Circles.
2. As you inhale, your palms are facing your chest and circling inward.
3. As you exhale, your palms are facing the floor and circling out away from your body. There is a slight feeling of pushing an object away with your palms as you exhale during this exercise.

Palms Circle the Earth

1. The next exercise is the same as Arm Circles, only your palms are facing the ground instead of your chest.
2. Stay relaxed. If your arms get tired, rest them at your sides and shake them. Then resume the exercises.

Raising Palms Up— Sinking Palms Down

1. Let your upper arms drop to your sides and bend your elbows so that your forearms and hands are directly in front of you and parallel to the floor.
2. As your legs bend and you inhale, let your forearms and hands rise up six to twelve inches with your palms facing upward.
3. Turn your wrists so your palms are facing the floor.
4. Straighten your legs and exhale, allowing your forearms and hands to sink to their original position. Your elbows should still be bent and your forearms approximately parallel to the floor.
5. Keep a slow, gentle, steady rhythm to your movement and breathing.

Sweeping the Floor

1. Turn your torso to the left, inhale and straighten up.
2. Exhale, dropping back down over the left foot; sweep the floor with your hands, turning to the right, and inhale and raise up over the right foot.
3. Drop back down over the right foot as you exhale and repeat the exercise.

Oval Circling in Front

1. Drop your hands to your sides and spread your legs so your feet are 20 inches apart.
2. Bend forward at the waist and let your arms swing down and out in front of you.
3. Exhale as you bend and drop.
4. Inhale up, straightening at the waist, and bring your hands up to the level of your eyes. Your hands, palms down, should be following an imaginary circle out in front of you.
5. Repeat the exercises and end bent at the waist with your arms and hands dangling.

Body Twists—Arms Swing

1. Rise back up, straightening at the waist, and assume the position used in Belly Breathing: knees bent, feet shoulder-width apart, lower back relaxed, and head and eyes looking straight forward.
2. With your feet planted firmly on the ground, sink your weight into your legs.
3. Twist at the waist allowing your arms to flop loosely around your body.
4. As you torque left and then right, let your hands slap your sides and back. Slowly increase the speed of your twisting motion until your hands are slapping your shoulders.
5. Continue to breathe and gently slow your twisting until your hands are slapping your buttocks and finally stop.

Energy Bounce

1. Using the same beginning position as in Body Twists, begin to bounce up and down on your center line.
2. As you bounce, move your attention through your body, relaxing any tight or stiff areas. First relax your calves; now thighs; relax your buttocks; now lower back; now upper back; relax your arms and shoulders and finally your neck and head.
3. Continue to bounce and breathe for another minute.
4. Relax; take three deep breaths and see how much energy you have.

As you complete these exercises, think about how you can carry this relaxed calm motion, deep breathing, and vital energy into all the activities of your day.

VII

Relaxation
and Energy

RELAXATION AND ENERGY

with Dani Riggs

TOO MUCH PRESSURE and tension can damage our vitality. Of course, some amount of personal drive is necessary for a productive life, and there will always be societal tensions, but for health there has to be a balance between effort and stress, on the one hand, and rest and relaxation on the other. Most of us are strongly affected by these ever-present individual and social pressures, and yet we don't know how to properly balance them. We don't know how to put energy back into our systems, circulate or channel it fully, and then return a giving flow to others. We need to learn ways that not only enable us to compensate for what we lose from stress, but that go further to develop strong, vibrant health.

When people are under a lot of pressure, either from internal or external conflicts, they get charged up for action. This is a normal physiological response that provides us with extra energy to handle a situation by automatically shifting our metabolism into a higher gear. These days we aren't facing the physical dangers that require this shift, but unfortunately, our bodies still automatically provide it. By constantly "revving our motors,"

emotional stress can wear us out. It can become a chronic problem if we are constantly under a lot of stress, especially if we have difficulty letting go of these pressures.

The Greater Energy program is not only easy but a safe and effective practice for relieving stress and tension. There are no dangers if you use common sense and understand the principles of relaxation. The harder and longer you do an exercise, the more you need to relax afterward. If you do these exercises and do not allow time to completely relax, then complications can occur. The exercises are very powerful, and the deep relaxation is a complementary balance just as important as the exercises themselves. Be sure to leave yourself plenty of time at the end of your sessions to gain the full benefits of this deeply relaxing and healing state.*

This chapter introduces basic techniques for utilizing relaxation and breathing to gain greater energy and to reduce stress. Simple routines are shown that can be done either sitting or standing.

Stress can literally drain our energy. Taking time each day to relax,

*For a guided deep relaxation, see page 53 in Chapter V.

set our focus away from our problems and practice a few Greater Energy breathing exercises can dramatically reduce our tension levels and eliminate the harmful effects of stress. Proper breathing is the most important key for enabling the system to fully relax and utilize the benefits of relaxation.

Our breathing is closely linked to our emotional state. Frustration or anger causes short, shallow, rapid breathing; fear tends to stop the flow of breathing; and worry leads to shallow, uneven breathing patterns. By changing our breathing to a full and relaxed pattern we can calm our emotions, helping to restore greater energy and harmony to our lives.

Posture is also important for attaining greater energy. Improper posture can cramp organs and impair their function. If we sit slouched, the lungs are compressed and our digestive organs are compacted into a small space. If we sit with too much backward curve, the kidneys are squeezed and the digestive organs are over-stretched. How can we expect our organs to function properly when there is not enought room for them to

move? Our posture also affects and reflects how we feel. When we are depressed or sad, we tend to collapse in the middle; when angry or frightened, we become rigid and our muscles become tense. Improving our posture helps to make us feel better. The exercises in this chapter will emphasize an upright, relaxed and open posture for comfort and ease.

Research in the United States, China and Japan has shown that there are multiple benefits from relaxation and breathing exercises. Alpha waves, a measure of the state of relaxation, increase. Oxygen consumption and metabolic rates are reduced. Blood laxtate levels, associated with muscle tension, drop. The heart rate is slowed, but blood circulation throughout the body and capillary action are increased. The rhythmic breathing pattern stimulates the digestive organs, increasing the absorption of nutrients and promoting the elimination functions of the body. By taking time to let go of the tensions in our life, relax and focus on our breathing, we can restore our health and revitalize our energy.

Energized Sitting

1. Sit on the edge of a chair. Choose a chair that will give you firm support and is high enough so that your thighs are parallel to the ground.

2. Place your feet shoulder-width apart, flat on the ground. Your feet should be parallel to each other. Look down at your feet and imagine railroad tracks running along their inside surface.

3. Your sitting posture should form three right angles. The first is between the floor and your lower leg. The second is between your lower leg and your thigh, and the third is between your thigh and your back.

4. Allow your hands to rest gently in your lap.

5. Imagine that someone is firmly pulling your hair from a point on top of your head and directly behind the ears. The upward lift creates just enough pull to help straighten the spine. Tilt your head with your chin to your throat so that you are looking toward the ground, about three feet directly in front of you. If you were facing a mirror you would be looking at your own legs.

6. Starting with your feet, concentrate on relaxing your entire body for two minutes. Close your eyes, take a few deep breaths and silently tell yourself to relax your legs, relax your thighs, relax your back, allow your arms and shoulders to relax, let your neck relax, and feel your eyes relax. Just let yourself completely relax.

7. Begin breathing in a full and relaxed manner. As you inhale, expand your lower abdomen, and as you exhale, gently contract your lower abdomen. To help slow your breathing, you may find it helpful to count slowly to five as you inhale and again slowly to five as you exhale. Do not strain or force your breath. Each breath should be full and relaxed.

8. Align your teeth so that the lower front teeth are lightly touching the upper front teeth. Place your tongue on your palate (the roof of the mouth) just behind the upper front teeth.

9. Find a focal point directly in front of you. Slowly draw that focal point in and gently close your eyes. Allow your attention to move down your centerline, through your heart, and focus on an area three inches below your navel and two inches inside. This area should correspond to the area of expansion and contraction that you are using for breathing in step seven.

10. Clear your mind and allow yourself to relax, breathe and focus your attention on your lower abdominal area, below the navel. If stray thoughts pop up, allow them to drift away. You can remain in this position for anywhere from three to thirty minutes. The greatest benefits are achieved with sessions of fifteen minutes or longer.

11. When you are ready to stop, slowly bring your focus up from your center through your heart, and gently open your eyes.

A Standing Alternative

For those of you who are interested in carrying this exercise further and for achieving greater results, there is a similar procedure done in a standing posture. When using the standing posture it is recommended that you start with a sitting session of at least five minutes. This allows you to begin relaxation and gain a feeling of calm before trying the standing method.

1. After completing a sitting session, gently lean forward and rise to a standing position. Your feet have not moved so they are still parallel and shoulder-width apart. Place your weight evenly on both feet.
2. Relax so that all the joints bend. The ankles should be loose and relaxed. Bend the knees by gently tucking and rotating the pelvis. This will help to straighten the curve in the lower back. Let your hands and arms hang loosely at your side.
3. Relax the pelvis, buttocks and anus.
4. Then proceed with steps five to eleven for the sitting exercise.

VIII

How to Overcome Fatigue

HOW TO OVERCOME FATIGUE

FATIGUE IS A CONDITION that can be caused by various imbalances, including physical deficiencies and excesses, dietary habits, emotional problems, and stagnant mental outlooks. By working on yourself on different levels you can begin to reverse the processes that cause fatigue. You can free yourself to experience both short-and long-range improvements in your vitality.

Physical Deficiencies

Three deficiencies that cause fatigue are (1) a lack of fresh air, and lack of deep ventilation of the lungs; (2) a lack of the vital energy through the acupressure points and meridians; and (3) inadequate circulation of the blood. Muscular tension in various degrees increases all these problems. By *releasing* tension, however, you can open up your system, and begin to free yourself from fatigue.

Proper Breathing

Many people spend a lot of their time indoors, both at work and at home, and therefore get very little fresh air. Even if you live in an area that suffers from air pollution, it is better to get outside at least sometime during the day to get away from the stagnant, and often dried-out indoor air.

How you breathe is important, as well as *what* you breathe. Tight chest muscles constrict the ribs so that they cannot work properly; many people breathe only shallowly. When this tension begins to be released, however, the chest can open the lungs more completely, resulting in deep, full breathing, a greater oxygenation of the blood, and increased vitality.

Many people only take deep breaths when they yawn, by which time they're already fatigued! Yawning is a reflex action whereby the body *forces* a deep breath to exhale stale air and get more oxygen to the blood. If you're not sure how deep or shallow your breathing is, take a yawn and feel how long and deep a breath it makes. Is yawning the only way *you* usually breathe deeply?

If so, deeper breathing alone can greatly increase your energy level, and can also help you relax. Many people are on a seesaw between pushing themselves and collapsing with fatigue.

It's wonderful to begin the process of replacing these negative extremes with the many rejuvenating methods and routines contained in this book.*

Vital Life Energy

The Chinese traditionally believe that we are born with a finite amount of energy, the amount depending generally on the state of health of our parents, and even of our ancestors. Further, we can either retain that inherited energy, deplete it, or increase it through the way we live. Factors that can affect the level of our energy are eating, exercise and breathing habits; mental and emotional conditions; deleterious habits, such as smoking, drinking and taking drugs; and environmental conditions, such as air quality and noise pollution.

When this energy is depleted by unhealthy living habits, there is less vital energy flowing through the acupressure points and meridians. This in turn has a negative effect on the internal organs, and lowers our resistance to disease in general.

But when we work to build up a strong energy reserve, we can strengthen and revitalize our organs, as well as our overall resistance. We can accomplish this through good diet, exercise, *Tai Chi*, deep breathing, acupressure and acu-yoga.

---

*Note: The standing exercises on pages 66-69 work well for relieving fatigue and general stress.

Improving Circulation

Poor circulation can result in undernourishment of the cells and tissues, since the nutrients in the blood cannot reach the cells as fully as possible and the toxic by-products of the cell metabolism cannot be completely carried away and excreted. Stagnation and tension in the area are the result.

Muscular tension decreases circulation and blocks deep breathing. It's invigorating to experience the process of erasing muscular tension, and the expansion of health and vitality that results from the Greater Energy techniques.

Conditions of Excess

Excesses, as well as deficiencies, can cause a lack of energy. Many people tend to push themselves too hard, to end up "running on nervous energy." But you can only push yourself so far before you snap. We aren't built to withstand more than a certain amount of stress. We each have to determine for ourselves how much is too much. Everybody has different stress limitations and overload levels. When you tune into yourself and cultivate your inner awareness, you can discover what is your optimum balance of activity and rest.

Traditionally, the Chinese discovered that excesses of particular activities weaken or damage particular organ meridians:

- Excess standing damages the Kidney Meridian
- Excess sitting damages the Spleen Meridian
- Excess lying down damages the Lung Meridian
- Excess looking damages the Heart Meridian
- Excess physical exertion damages the Liver Meridian

You might want to work on points, for example on the Kidney Meridian, if you have to stand up a lot. Many occupations demand that people do an excessive amount of standing, sitting, or using the eyes. It's important to counteract these stresses in order to prevent fatigue.

TECHNIQUES FOR RELIEVING FATIGUE

Foot Massage

Foot massage is an excellent way of overcoming fatigue and restoring vitality. Take off your shoes and socks. Firmly massage the ankles and the arches of both feet. Next massage the soles of the feet and the toes. Half of the organ meridians run through the feet, especially through the toes.

When you massage your feet, be sure to work on Kidney 1, the first point on the Kidney Meridian, located on the sole at the bottom of the ball of the foot (see photo). This point, called "Bubbling Spring," is an acupressure first-aid revival point. It's a source of energy for the entire body, and provides a quick way to pick yourself up from a state of fatigue.

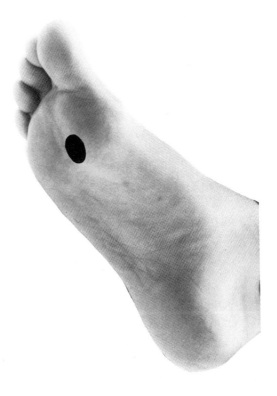

Spinal Rocking

Rocking on your spine is another easy technique for relieving fatigue, and one that works on different aspects of the body. First, of course, it provides a good massage for the spine, the back muscles, and all the acupressure points that run alongside the spine. All the nerves stemming out of the spine are related to all the organs, as are the acupressure points on the spinal muscles, so rocking on the spine is actually a whole-body treatment.

Second, spinal rocking works on tension in the neck and shoulder area, which can also cause fatigue. By rocking all the way up onto your shoulders and neck, you press the muscles and points there, releasing tightness.

Third, during the spinal rocking the hands are placed on a specific acupressure point, Stomach 36. This

point has certain traditional associations: it helps strengthen all the muscles, and is the most widely used point for revitalizing the whole body.

Stomach 36 is called "Sanri," which means "Three More Miles." Its muscle

strengthening qualities work for greater endurance. Athletes, hikers, and backpackers can use this strong acupressure point as a tonic to release physical fatigue.

Sanri, or The Three Mile Point, is located on the outer side of the lower leg, just below the knee. One way to find it is: (1) Sit in a chair with your knees at right angles. (2) Put your left palm over the front of the left knee. (3) With your fingers spread comfortably, your ring finger will be on the point. Press the muscle there at a 90 degree angle from the surface of the skin.

The combination of stimulating various back, neck, and shoulder points while holding *Sanri*, makes spinal rocking an especially effective exercise for physical rejuvenation.

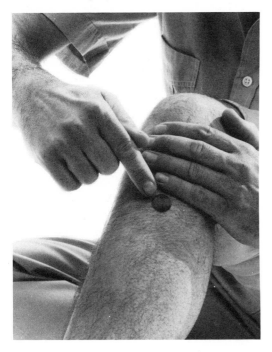

Dietary Considerations

The foods you eat affect your energy level. Poor nutrition starves the body of the building blocks—protein, carbohydrates, fat, vitamins, minerals, and fiber—that it requires to function properly. This can fatigue the body. Therefore, if you *don't* eat nourishing food, and *do* eat items that actively detract from health and well-being, you shouldn't be surprised if you have a problem with lack of energy.

Salt and sugar, for example, are two substances which many people consume excessively. Processed foods usually contain one or the other, if not both. Salt and sugar both can cause fatigue by creating biochemical imbalances. Sugar depletes the body of vitamins, and strains the pancreas, which has a more difficult job of balancing the blood sugar level when sugar is eaten. Salt throws off the body's water balance so that more water is required, but more is also retained in the body. Salt also tends to have a binding or constricting effect on the muscles.

Another dietary problem related to fatigue is overeating, or eating heavy, rich foods. This puts a strain on the digestive system, since it takes extra energy to cope with the overload, thus depleting your available energy. And when your internal organs are tired, so are you.

Fatigue can also be a symptom of overall nutritional deficiencies—of vitamins, minerals, or protein, for example. By eating fresh, unprocessed, and easily digestible foods, however, you can create healthy, well-nourished internal organs.

Emotional Considerations

A lack of energy can also indicate emotional imbalances. If you repress your feelings, you create muscle tension and tightness (in order to literally "hold the lid on"), and you also limit your experience of your life.

One way you can begin to unblock yourself is through visualization, by opening your mind and imagination. Many people avoid their feelings, thereby deadening themselves, so that their lives are dull and boring.

You can begin to turn boredom around, however, by using your imagination to explore various possible ways of being and doing new things. You can open yourself to a new sense of vitality and fulfillment; you can begin to get in touch with deep feelings about what you need and want in life; you can visualize what you want to happen and create a new reality; you *can make* your dreams come true.

Mental Considerations

Our minds have tremendous power to influence our lives—more than we are usually led to believe. What we perceive, what we visualize or project to a large extent determines what we get. Our thoughts create our reality by creating *how we perceive* reality.

In this context, it's possible to see how our minds can create fatigue. For example, we may wake up feeling refreshed, but when we look at the clock and see that we had only seven hours of sleep instead of our usual eight, we may then feel tired. Fatigue can also be a mental response to doing something we don't want to do. The following quote explains other instances of mentally-created fatigue:

Tiredness is geared to three causes: loss of energy, which is the chief reason, and besides this, excess of activity of mind and of body. One generally knows tiredness to be caused by excess of bodily activity, but one is apt to overlook the fact that excess of activity of the mind also causes tiredness.

The activities that especially cause tiredness are worry, fear, anxiety, and pain. There is, however, one mental cause that is less obvious, and that is the thought of being tired. Among a hundred cases of tired people, you will find 90 cases of this particular kind of tiredness. When a person thinks 'I am tired,' the very thought creates the feeling of tiredness in support of the thought, and the reason brings forward a thousand reasons that seem to have caused the tiredness. There are some who think that the presence of people, or of some people, or the presence of a particular person tires them; some think that their energy, their life, is eaten up by some people; some think that a particular action takes away their energy; some think that strength is taken out of them by their everyday duties in life or by the work they happen to do, such as singing, speaking, doing bodily or mental work; and of course, as they think, so they experience.*

*Sufi Inayat Khan, The Book of Health, London, England: Sufi Publishing Co., 1974, 56-57.

IX

Resistance
to Illness

RESISTANCE TO ILLNESS

OUR DEGREE OF RESISTANCE to illness is in direct relationship with the balance, strength, and flexibility of our bodies. If we take care of ourselves by eating properly, getting enough rest and exercise, and by practicing techniques that release old tensions, then our resistance to illness is strong. If, on the other hand, we abuse our bodies, push ourselves too hard, eat badly, don't exercise, and don't involve ourselves with practices that release tension and enhance our energy, our resistance will be low, or weak, and we will be more prone to illness.

Fatigue is an important element in your resistance level. In this fast-paced society it is easy to overwork yourself, to take on too many commitments, to push yourself beyond your limits and into fatigue. This imbalance has a weakening effect on all parts of the body.

When we get enough rest, however, we give our bodies a chance to recover fully from our activities. Deep relaxation furthers the circulation of blood and nourishes the whole body, especially the internal organs.

Dietary Considerations

Diet also plays an important role in resistance to illness. When we eat processed, preserved, or devitalized foods, we weaken our system and our resistance. However, there are foods that strengthen the body and build resistance, reinforcing the body's ability to protect itself. Examples are miso soup, parsley, beans, tofu, sea vegetables, sauteed vegetables, and lightly toasted sesame seeds. (See the following chapter on Foods for Greater Energy.)

Acupressure Points

There is an acupressure point (B36), located near the spine off the tips of the shoulder blades, that governs resistance, especially resistance to colds and flus. The Chinese book, *The Yellow Emperor's Classic of Internal Medicine*, says that "wind and cold enter the pores of the skin" at this point. These points around the tips of the shoulder blades are the first to get blocked up just before an illness, especially a cold or flu, takes hold.

An ancient method for developing greater energy and maintaining resistance against illness is to swing a thick branch, golf club or baseball bat back and forth. The Yogis would do this when they felt any illness about to come on, since it was common knowledge that the tensions which accumulate between the shoulder blades contribute to illness. The swinging motion helped break down this tension. Swinging a golf club or a baseball bat around moves and stretches the shoulder blades to release the tensions that collect there.

The following Greater Energy exercise works on these points, directly pressing them as you lift your weight onto the tops of your shoulder blades.

Bridge Pose

1. Lie on your back.
2. Bend your knees so that the soles of your feet are flat on the floor.
3. Put your arms above your head on the floor and relax them.
4. Inhale, arching the pelvis up. Hold for several seconds.
5. Exhale as you slowly come down. Continue to inhale up and exhale down for one minute.
6. Relax on your back with your eyes closed for a few minutes.

Benefits: This exercise increases resistance to illness while relieving shoulder tension. It is helpful for balancing the thyroid, improving poor circulation and easing breathing difficulties.

X

Foods for
Greater Energy

FOODS FOR GREATER ENERGY

FOOD IS THE FUEL that generates energy for our bodies; exercise burns up this fuel. Thus, there is a direct link between what you eat, how you eat, and how much exercise you do. Exercise improves circulation, provides an outlet for physical, emotional, and mental tensions, and generally strengthens and tones all the body's muscles. All these aspects help improve your overall condition and digestion.

When you exercise regularly, you also tend to develop a healthy appetite, a positive frame of mind, and an overall increase in vitality. The tendency to get depressed or to overeat decreases when you put your body to work. Exercise naturally regulates your whole system. When you don't exercise, your metabolism can become sluggish. Improved digestion, assimilation, and elimination are just some of the benefits of the Greater Energy exercise routines combines with a balanced whole foods diet.

The Right Diet

There are as many dietary options as there are foods on the commercial market, and there is a spectrum of opinions on the right way to eat. But we are all individuals, and have differing nutritional needs.

The past and present course of our lives influences our dietary needs. Every person has a unique combination of past eating habits, parental influences, tastes, lifestyles, physical activity, climate and metabolism. This great diversity is matched by the diversity of dietary desires and requirements for each individual's optimum health.

There are tension-producing foods and tension-releasing foods. Eating a lot of salt, for example, has been shown to be directly related to high blood pressure. It hardens and constricts the arteries, impeding the blood flow. Thus, the heart must pump harder to circulate the blood through the restricted vessels. Salt tends to stiffen the muscles, creating muscular tensions which also hamper the blood flow. Meat, which contains both salt and animal fats, contributes to hypertension. Since virtually all canned, packaged, processed foods contain salt or white sugar (often both!), they should be avoided. These should be replaced by fresh vegetables and fruits, whole grains, and various other natural foods.

The best way to know what is the right diet for you is to experiment with and inform yourself* about a variety of ways of eating. *Experience for yourself* what effects different diets have on how you feel. Try different foods, quantities, combinations, ratios. This way you can learn what diet makes you feel best. Remember, however, that it can change! As the seasons change, our dietary needs change also.† Gradually change your diet; remember to use moderation, however, since extreme changes cause imbalances. And it takes a while to gain the benefits of changing your diet. Results don't happen overnight, although you may experience some immediate effects. Be patient and give your body time to adjust.

Food Combining

In order to obtain the most energy from the foods you eat, you need to know how to properly combine them; it's important to have an understanding about which foods work against each other and which are complementary for increasing digestion and your production of vital energy.

Principles of food combining are based on the fact that certain foods are digested differently than others, so that when they are eaten together neither one can be digested properly. Various foods require both different enzymes and different amounts of time

to be digested thoroughly. When eaten together they ferment, causing putrefaction in the digestive system.

It is best to avoid eating foods from these categories at the same time:
- Fruits with other foods (proteins, starches, vegetables)
- Melons with other foods (including other fruits)
- Different sources of proteins together (nuts, legumes, dairy products, meats)
- Proteins and starches

Good combinations are:
- Fruits with other fruits (except melons)
- Proteins with vegetables
- Starches with vegetables

Experiment with eating foods in proper combinations—you may be surprised at the results!

Abdominal Tension

The digestive organs are located in the abdominal area. Thus, digestion is affected by tension in the abdominal muscles and in the diaphragm, the muscle which separates the thoracic and abdominal cavities. When the digestive organs are subject to excess stress and tensions, their functioning can be hampered, causing indigestion and a poor assimilation of nutrients.

Tension in the abdominal muscles, in the diaphragm, or in the digestive organs themselves affects digestion no matter what, how, or how much you eat. Eventually, when enough tension

---

*Naboru Muramoto, Healing Ourselves, Avon Books, 1973.

†Elson M. Haas, M.D., Staying Healthy with the Seasons, Celestial Arts, 1981.

builds up in the area, the digestive process can be impaired. Indigestion, lethargy, sluggishness, belching or gas can be the result.

Abdominal tensions can produce a deep irritation in the pit of the stomach. This sometimes unconsciously drives a person to overeat, in an attempt to relieve that tension. In this case an acupressure point located in this area (Conception Vessel 12, between the navel and the base of the sternum) can be helpful in relieving the irritation. Gradually press into the pit of the stomach at a 45 degree angle toward the diaphragm. Through prolonged pressure on the lump lodged inside this abdominal point, blockages can be broken up and gas expelled.

When your abdominal muscles are relaxed and balanced, the stomach and intestines—which are muscles themselves—are free to work properly. As we breathe fully, the rhythmic movements made by the diaphragm internally massage the stomach. The abdomen needs to be firm (strong, not flabby), with good muscle tone, but also flexible (relaxed, not hard or rigid) to enable the digestive organs to function properly.

Both what we eat and how we eat are important components of the Greater Energy program. Some foods have a high concentration of energy within them, while other foods have been devitalized (e.g. from pesticide use, in the processing stage, etc.). The fresher, the more natural, and if cooked, the more it's prepared with love, the more energy your food will contain.

The following foods are noted for their natural abundance of nutritious minerals and vitamins. Although these foods are healthy and beneficial, it is important not to overeat them. Remember to use moderation. Even the greatest health-building food becomes toxic to our system if eaten in excess.

SOME MEDICINAL PROPERTIES OF COMMON FOODS

Aduki beans cooked with at least four times as much water produce a juice that benefits the kidneys. Take about a half-cup of this juice (warm) about an hour before your meal. Traditionally, aduki beans have been used for kidney and lower back trouble.

Alfalfa leaf is one of the best alkalizers known to man. It is rich in vitamin K, the blood-clotting agent, and in nitrogen, calcium, potassium, phosphorus, and magnesium. Eat the green alfalfa sprouts in salads and in sandwiches.

Beets are excellent for the liver. They help to cleanse the blood and to build red corpuscles. Beets are rich in manganese, and also contain potassium, iron, and sodium. Use the raw roots, grated fine, and the tops, ground and chopped, in salads.

Broccoli is a body cleanser and weight reducer. It contains high amounts of vitamin A, potassium, phosphorus, and sulfur. Eat it raw in salads or lightly steamed or sauteed.

Carrots are good for the liver and the spleen. Carrots are high in potassium, calcium, iron, magnesium, manganese, sulfur, chlorine, phosphorus, and protein.

Carrots contain a high concentration of vitamin A, which aids in cleansing the blood. Eaten raw, they are useful for beautification as aids for the skin. Carrots also strengthen your resistance to illness. They have traditionally been useful for night blindness, and have been given to children who wet their beds. The carrot tops are also eaten to enhance these benefits and for increasing a person's health and vitality.

Dong Quai root (available at most health food stores) is a famous Chinese medicine for the female reproductive system. It is used for building blood, nourishing the female glands, regulating monthly periods, and correcting menopausal symptoms, including hot flashes and spasms of the vagina. It is also used in anemic conditions in mothers after childbirth but is never given to women during pregnancy. It has also proved very helpful in amenorrhea (stoppage of normal monthly periods, scanty periods) and deficient secretion of uterine mucosa. Chinese herbalists advise that little or no fruit should be eaten while you take Dong Quai. Vegetables should be included in the diet, and a slice of ginger root should be cooked with them.

Ginger Juice is made by finely grating fresh ginger root and squeezing it through a cheese cloth. This stimulating juice is used in hot water to make special therapeutic hot compresses for muscular disorders. It can also be mixed into massage oil. Traditionally it is used internally in soups and other cooking to guard against sore throats, colds, and flus.

Ginger tea is excellent for soothing sore throats and helping to prevent the onset of a cold or flu. Try boiling several slices of fresh ginger in a pot for about 20 minutes. Add honey to taste, and milk (optional) for this traditional remedy.

Miso is a dark paste made from an aged mixture of soybeans and salt. It is used to make soups, sauces, and dips. This common Oriental food is widely used in traditional dietary therapy. There are three major types of miso: **Kome Miso** (rice added; the most mild); **Mugi Miso** (barley added); **Hacho Miso** (strong, high salt content).

The benefits of miso: Boiling miso destroys its nutrients and digestive enzymes. Always add the paste after cooking. Miso helps to restore the beneficial intestinal bacteria and aids in the digestion and assimilation of food. Miso also generally strengthens the metabolism and alkalizes the system. It is traditionally used for anemic and arthritic people.

Miso generally strengthens the whole body, improving resistance to colds and flus. Miso is known to have important digestive enzymes which benefit the intestines and aid in the assimilation of food.

Onion tonifies the reproductive systems. Buddhist monks do not eat meat or onions. Onions generate the sex drive. They are used to eliminate

roundworms. They may also make someone look thinner even when he/she eats a lot. The Chinese say that eating two eggs along with half of an onion every day for ten days will strengthen a person's overall condition. Onions are also good for the condition of the blood and therefore are used for weakness and fatigue.

Peas, eaten raw with their pods, are a tonifier for the pancreas. Peas are rich in potassium and magnesium and fairly high in protein.

Parsley is useful against inflammations of the kidneys, bladder, urethra, and genital organs. Parsley is a digestive stimulant and regulator of the liver and spleen, and is rich in potassium. Eat it raw in salads. Parsley aids in eliminating excessive uric acid and is excellent for reducing muscular tensions.

Parsley tea produces a soothing effect on the lining of the urinary passages. It is traditionally used for kidney and bladder irritation, congestion, inflammation, or weakness. Parsley tea is prepared by placing a fresh bunch of parsley in two pints of cold water. This is simmered not more than 10 seconds, removed from the burner and allowed to stand until cold. Four cups of the tea are taken daily.

Parsnips are good for the urinary system, bladder conditions, and kidney stones. Parsnips are rich in phosphorus, sulfur, silicon, potassium, and chlorine.

Rice (brown) is good for the lungs and large intestine. Soft brown rice is especially good for older people who have constipation. Brown rice has a high amount of vitamin B, and helps to strengthen the body. It's eaten to help prevent arterial sclerosis, constipation, diarrhea, and anemia. It is also good for women who cannot get pregnant. Brown rice can be useful in preventing obesity, hemorrhoids and diabetes.

Royal Jelly is produced and collected by worker bees. The queen bee receives royal jelly in this way throughout her life. She lays approximately one-quarter of a million eggs during the mating season. Worker bees do not consume royal jelly and only live for two to six months. The queen bee lives as long as eight years. Increased energy and considerable memory improvement have been reported about royal jelly.

Seaweeds are an excellent source of natural minerals and vitamins. They help to strengthen the overall condition of the body. When eaten in moderation a couple of times a week, the following seaweeds (available at most health food stores) can give your body the proper nutrition it needs to produce greater levels of energy.

Hijiki–can be an excellent substitute for pasta. Soak or boil it for 15 minutes. It makes a great salad with parsley, scallions, and tofu in a garlic dressing. It is also good in a thick spaghetti sauce with cauliflower and zucchini. Try making a sauté of soaked hijiki with burdock, a little ginger, and lotus root. Add soy sauce (to taste) toward the end of the cooking.

Kombu–this variety of seaweed is especially rich in natural minerals and vitamins. Traditionally it has been used for arthritis, and high and low blood pressure. Try soaking it, then cook along with vegetables, especially carrots or squash added to brown rice or millet.

Wakame–is packed with organic minerals and vitamins. It is excellent in miso soup.

Kanten–made from agar seaweed, is a good low calorie dessert for obesity and compulsive eating. Boil the agar in water until it melts. Then add any of the following for flavoring: lemon rind or juice, currants, raisins, figs, cinnamon or apple juice.

Spinach is one of the most nourishing foods for all of the cells, tissues, nerves, and muscles. It contains the finest quality of organic iron obtainable, and is rich in sodium, potassium, calcium, and magnesium. Raw spinach builds *chi* when eaten regularly.

HOW TO GAIN THE MAXIMUM ENERGY FROM THE FOODS YOU EAT

Relaxation before and during eating promotes good digestion. Five long, deep breaths, preferably with your eyes closed, before eating helps to relax you, and create a receptive mood in which to enjoy your meal.

Give Thanks to life for the earth, all the natural processes, cycles, and human efforts that went into creating and cultivating the food you are about to eat. If you learn to appreciate what you have before you, your positive attitude of gratitude will enable you to receive its nourishment and be revitalized more fully.

Eat Slowly—Chew Completely. This cannot be overemphasized! Hurried eating and incomplete chewing contribute to indigestion in a number of ways:

1. They can indicate an imbalanced state of tension, anxiety and rushing. This practically guarantees some degree of indigestion. If you only have a small amount of time in which to eat, eat only a small amount of food, and chew it slowly and completely.
2. Incomplete chewing hinders digestion because the enzymes in the saliva that begin the digestion process while the food is being chewed don't get a chance to do their job. This puts an added burden on the stomach.
3. When you eat quickly, you often overeat because you don't give your system the opportunity to signal that it's full. And when you do notice that you're full, you're often noticing that you're already stuffed!
4. Hurried eating means that you aren't really tasting whatever it is you're gobbling down, and so you aren't even getting the satisfaction of good taste out of your food. Deep breathing and thorough chewing will enhance the flavors of your food and will probably enable you to eat less while getting more gratification out of your meals.

Meditation and Deep Breathing Before Eating:

In a sitting position, grasp your legs just above your knees and sit up straight. Close your eyes. Breathe in six times, through your mouth, swallowing the air each time. Hold the breath and slightly rotate your hips and abdomen ten times. Straighten your spine and exhale. Then reverse the direction of the rotation, and repeat the entire exercise five times, rotating in each direction.

Finish the exercise by taking three long, deep breaths. Tune into your whole body. Mentally prepare yourself to be grateful for the food you have before you. Open your eyes. Enjoy.

RECIPES FOR GREATER ENERGY

Greater Energy Foods

Proper cooking, using quality ingredients and balanced proportions in combining foods, can increase the available energy in the foods you eat. Cooking in this way can enable your body to digest and assimilate the nutrients maximally.

If you overcook your food, you can kill its life-force properties. The vitamins and minerals contained in green vegetables, for instance, along with their chlorophyl content, can be depleted by overcooking.

The quality of the foods you eat is also important for assimilating greater energy. Fresh foods, of course, are more nutritious than old food which has been depleted of its vitality. Organic foods, grown in richer soil without harmful chemicals like pesticides, contain greater concentrations of vitamins and minerals than commercially grown foods.

An increased consciousness about how and what you eat is essential for enhanced vitality in your daily life. Attention to balanced protein combinations, cooking time, even the colors of your food, can make a tremendous difference in nurturing your body effectively.

The following recipes have been formulated with ingredients that naturally fortify the body with greater energy. Many of these delicious dishes contain rich, potent foods which should not be overeaten. In fact, you will often get more energy out of these recipes if you eat them in moderation and get a full half-hour of exercise during the day. When you consistently eat these greater energy foods and practice the self-help exercises in this book, you will become more healthy, peaceful and alive with vital energy.

Potency Soup

(*Start the night before*)

A thick, slightly salty, rich bean soup is a well known Oriental folk remedy for sexual reproductive weaknesses, impotency, and general fatigue. Azuki (small red beans) and black beans are especially good for increasing energy and sexual appetite. Eating a combination of three parts grain to one part beans not only complements all of the essential amino acids for a complete protein, but also helps to stabilize the sexual hormones and produce energy for the body to store.

1 tbsp. sesame oil
1 tsp. finely chopped garlic
2 cups chopped onion
1 cup diced celery
1 cup diced carrots
1 cup chopped tomatoes (fresh or canned)
1 tsp. basil
½ tsp. thyme
½ cup small white beans
½ cup pinto beans
½ cup black beans
1 cup mung beans
1 cup kidney beans
½ cup chopped parsley
10 cups water
¼ cup soy sauce or tamari
salt and pepper to taste

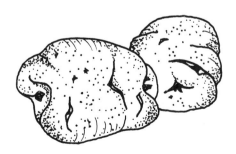

Soak the beans overnight in a large bowl with plenty of water. Heat the oil in a saucepan. Add garlic and onion to sauté for 5 minutes. Then add the carrots, celery, tomatoes, basil, thyme and chopped parsley for 5 more minutes.

Add the beans, water, salt and pepper, and bring to a boil. Reduce the heat and simmer for 1 hour. Then add salt and simmer with the cover on for another hour. Taste, season and serve with whole grain toast.

Miso Vegetable Soup

(45 *minutes to prepare*)

1 tbsp. sesame oil
2 large onions, diced
4 cloves minced garlic
¼ tsp. basil
seasalt and pepper to taste
2 celery stalks
5 tomatoes
2 large carrots
1 cup fresh broccoli
2 medium zucchini
2 tbsp. miso paste

Heat the sesame oil in a large kettle. Add the onions, celery and garlic. Sauté with spices for five minutes.

Add all the chopped vegetables and cover with water or vegetable broth. Simmer for ten minutes.

Turn off the heat. Dilute 2 tbsp. of miso with several tbsp. of hot broth, and add to the soup. Stir well, and serve immediately.

Broccoli Boost

(Takes ½ hour)

2 carrots, sliced thin
2 or 3 broccoli spears, cut into bite-size
   pieces
3 tomatoes, sliced into wedges
¼ head of red cabbage (diced)
¼ lb. Monterey Jack cheese, grated
   (optional)
Italian, garlic or herbal salad dressing
1 cup whole raw almonds

Preheat oven to 350 degrees. Spread almonds on a cookie sheet or pie plate and roast them in the oven for 15 minutes or until lightly brown. While still hot, place the almonds in a bowl and immediately pour one tablespoon of tamari (soy sauce) over the almonds. Stir and let sit while you prepare the salad.

Cut the raw vegetables and mix them in a large salad bowl. Grate the cheese and sprinkle on top. Pour the dressing of your choice on top and toss. Sprinkle the roasted almonds on top just before serving.

Served with fresh bread, toast or crackers, this can make an excellent energy-enhancing meal for two people. This recipe serves four as a side dish.

Casserole Variation: Try this dish heated. Just dice an onion and mix a can of tomato sauce with the above ingredients. Sprinkle with cheese, cover and bake at 350 degrees for 15 to 20 minutes. Sprinkle the freshly roasted almonds on top just before serving.

Hot and Sour Soup

(Takes 1 hour to prepare)

Sauté the following in one tablespoon sesame oil:

2 cloves minced garlic
½ tsp. freshly grated ginger
2 onions, diced
2 celery sticks, chopped

Add the above to 10 cups of water or vegetable stock. Bring to a boil and then simmer for 30 minutes with:

2 carrots, chopped
2 yams, chopped
½ cup split peas or lentils

Then add the following ingredients and simmer 10 minutes longer:

¼ cup rice vinegar
½ cup Wakame or hijiki seaweed*
¼ cup tamari or soy sauce
¼ tsp. black pepper

Stir in 2 beaten eggs. Add a tablespoon of roasted sesame oil to the soup. Serve topped with minced scallions.

These seaweeds, high in calcium and iron, are available at most health food stores and Oriental food sections of supermarkets.

Vitality Sauce

(One hour to prepare; serves 4 people)

1 cup peanut butter
2 cups chopped onion
3 cloves crushed garlic
2 tbsp. honey
1 tsp. fresh grated ginger
juice of one lemon
2 cups water
2 tbsp. tamari or soy sauce
2 tbsp. sesame oil

Sauté the onions, garlic and ginger in oil for 5 to 6 minutes. Add the remaining ingredients, stir, and simmer with a very low heat for 30 minutes. Serve with freshly cooked vegetables and brown rice.

Crisp Nut Salad

(soak one cup of raw peanuts overnight)

To prepare for the salad, drain the water from the peanuts, recover with fresh water, and store in the refrigerator.

3 stalks celery
2 tomatoes
2 carrots
1 cup cabbage
2 green onions
1 bunch parsley

Dice the vegetables and stir together with the cup of soaked peanuts. Toss with an oil and vinegar dressing.

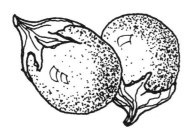

Vital Steamed Greens

Lightly cooked green vegetables are an essential dietary component to eat daily for obtaining greater energy. Green vegetables contain high amounts of energy from the sun in the form of chlorophyl.

If you properly cook green vegetables, their color will become a vibrant, rich green. Leafy vegetables require only a few minutes of cooking to soften their outer protective layers, making them easier to digest but still retaining their valuable nutrients and healing chlorophyl.

The following leafy greens are an excellent source of Vitamin B and are important to eat several times a week for greater energy.

- Broccoli
- Beet Tops
- Bok Choy
- Kale
- Swiss Chard
- Spinach

Choose one or two of these vital greens. Thoroughly wash and chop them into bite size pieces. Bring one cup of water to a simmer in a stainless steel pot and steam the greens for three minutes or until they become a vibrant, dark green. Immediately toss them in the following light, tasty sauce.

2 tbsp. soy sauce or tamari
2 tbsp. lemon juice
2 tbsp. sesame oil
dash of pepper or onion powder (optional)

Quick Energy Sprouts

(*10 minutes to prepare; serves* 4)

Try this dish when you don't have much time to cook, want to eat light, and want extra energy. This recipe is diuretic, can relieve hypertension, and is highly beneficial for the nervous system.

2 sticks of celery, chopped
2 cups of fresh bean sprouts
1 bunch of green onions, chopped
2 tbsp. sesame oil
dash of pepper
1 tbsp. soy sauce or tamari

In a wok or large frying pan, heat the sesame oil. Then add the celery, sprouts and green onions, stirring and tossing constantly for only one minute. Turn off the heat, add the pepper and soy sauce, stir well and serve immediately.

Sweet Energy Bars

(*1½ hours to prepare, including baking*)

¾ cup orange juice
2 cups pitted dates
1 cup water
small pinch of salt

Slowly simmer the dates in salted water for 5 minutes. Use a fork to mash the dates while they are cooking. Mix in the orange juice and set aside.

1 cup whole wheat pastry flour
½ cup bran
1 cup rolled oats
½ cup sesame seeds
½ cup melted butter or oil
1 cup hot water

Preheat oven to 325 degrees. Mix the flour, bran, oats and seeds together in a bowl. Stir in the melted butter or oil and hot water.

Grease a square baking pan (8- or 9-inch). Then press one third of the flour mixture into the bottom of the pan. Layer one half of the date mixture. Then add another one-third portion of the flour mixture followed by the rest of the dates. Top with the final third of the oat mixture. Firmly press these layers down to enable it to hold together. Bake for 50 minutes.

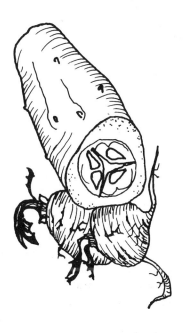

Greater Energy Cookies

(1½ hours preparation, including baking)

These high protein cookies are high in calcium and B vitamins. For this reason, they are good for helping to prevent PMS and menstrual cramps. They also make a great high energy, quick, nutritious snack.

1½ cups sesame seeds
1 cup raisins (chopped in small pieces)
2 cups whole wheat flour
4 eggs
1 cup Tahini
1 cup barley-corn malt
¼ cup molasses
2 tsp. vanilla
1 tsp. salt
½ tsp. cinnamon
water

Lightly roast the flour in a dry pan until it smells toasty. Turn off the heat and add the sesame seeds, salt and cinnamon to the flour. Mix the remaining ingredients in a large bowl. Slowly mix in the flour mixture. Add just enough water to make a thick, stiff batter.

Preheat the oven to 325 degrees. Grease a couple of cookie sheets. Spoon the batter to form ¼-inch thick cookies. Bake for 30 minutes or until lightly browned.

Sweet Tofu Pie

(2½ hours, including baking; serves 8)

Pie crust ingredients:
1½ cups whole wheat flour
½ cup sesame seeds or wheat germ
1 tsp. salt (optional)
10 tbsp. margarine or butter
5 to 6 tbsp. ice cold water

Mix the flour, seeds, wheat germ and salt together. Then mash the margarine or butter into the dry ingredients. Use your hand to form dough into a ball. Cover and refrigerate for at least a half-hour. Roll out dough on a lightly floured surface. Then carefully transfer into a greased pie plate. Preheat oven to 350 degrees.

Filling:
1 pound firm tofu
2 cups baked yams
2 eggs
½ cup honey or 1 cup barley malt syrup
½ tsp. cinnamon
½ tsp. salt
½ cup raw whole almonds

Slice tofu ¼ inch thick and evenly spread the pieces over the dough. Peel and mash the yams. Beat the eggs and mix the yams, eggs, honey or barley syrup, cinnamon and salt together in a bowl. Pour the yam mixture over the layer of tofu and even the top of the pie smoothly with the back of a spoon. Press the almonds into the yam, making a pattern. Bake for an hour. Thoroughly cool before serving.

GLOSSARY

Acupressure: A method of bodywork that uses the Chinese system of acupuncture points and meridians combined with Japanese finger pressure techniques to release muscular tensions.

Acupuncture: A traditional method of Chinese medicine in which fine needles are inserted into the body in key points to release internal blockages and balance energy.

Acu-Yoga: An integration of acupressure and yoga used for self-treatment.

Affirmations: Personal statements said aloud or thought to oneself that positively validate different aspects of one's existence. They are used to creatively enable one to visualize and increase the benefits of acu-yoga techniques.

Blockage: An accumulation or congestion of energy in or surrounding an acupressure point. Blockages in a meridian may ache, be painful, or feel numb before manifesting as a physical symptom.

Breathing awareness: The ability to deepen and direct the breath into different parts of the body through concentration and relaxation.

Centering: The process of gaining awareness of the mind and body. This enables a person to be more conscious in the present moment.

Chakra: A vital center for giving and receiving life energy. Chakras are anatomically identified with the nerve plexuses of the body.

Chi: A Chinese word for vital energy. It has been translated as "material energy" or "vital matter" which circulates through the meridians.

Chronic muscular tension: A long-term condition in which the muscle fibers are held indefinitely in a shortened, contracted state.

Deep Relaxation: The letting go of all parts of the body and mind to allow a natural flow of energy to circulate in its natural course. To completely relax after strenuous exercise is the best way to recharge the nervous system.

Disease: An imbalance in the system as a whole.

Energy: The basis of all forms of life and matter in the universe. It is a dynamic force that circulates through the body in specific pathways called meridians.

Energy blockage: An obstruction to the free flow of vital matter which manifests physically as tension, pain, or stiffness. Thoughts and emotions can also cause energy blockages.

Grounded: The experience of being connected with the Earth.

Holistic: An approach to life based on a perspective that all forms of existence are unified, that the whole equals more than the sum of its parts, and that every aspect, whether internal or external, affects the whole.

Homeostatic: A mechanism of equilibrium or balance.

Hypertension: Abnormally high arterial blood pressure.

Hyperventilation: Heavy breathing through the mouth, which results in an excessive intake of oxygen and elimination of carbon dioxide from the blood, causing nausea or extreme dizziness.

Intuition: The inner guidance of meaningful thought and impressions.

Jin Shin: A highly developed acupressure massage technique which uses gentle-to-deep finger pressure applied to specific points on the human anatomy. This system releases tension and rebalances all areas of the body.

Ki: The Japanese word for the vital life energy which concentrates in all living things. It circulates through the human body in pathways called meridians.

Life Force: The vital energy contained in all things. The three main types are: (1) the energy that circulates through the body via the meridians; (2) the power generated from the human qualities of love, devotion, determination, will-power and positive thinking or projection; and (3) the forces of nature which include the wind, rain, sun, heat, magnetism, gravity, and electricity.

Lumbar: The last five vertebrae before the sacrum on the lower back.

Mantra: Sounds which are used repeatedly during meditation to affect higher states of consciousness.

Meditation: Focusing one's attention for developing the spiritual capabilities of the mind.

Meridians: The pathways along which energy flows through the body, connecting the various acupressure/acupuncture points. The internal organs named after each meridian are abbreviated as follows: Lung (LU); Spleen (Sp); Heart (H); Kidney (K); Triple Warmer (TW); Liver (Lv); Conception Vessel (CV); Large intestine (LI); Stomach (St); Small Intestine (SI); Bladder (B); Pericardium (P); Gall Bladder (GB); Governing Vessel (GV).

Movement Therapy: Utilizing dance and creative movements as a form of self-healing.

Mudras: Easy hand positions which produce electrical currents through the meridians.

Nervous System: The network of nerves which regulates muscular functioning. It influences the coordination of every cell, organ, and system in the body with one's environment.

Nei Ching, The Yellow Emperor's Classic of Internal Medicine: An important traditional Chinese medical book written in 2697 B.C. by Huang Ti, the Yellow Emperor.

Prana: The essential life force which circulates in the air, food, plants, and in the human body. It is the life behind the atom, found in all forms of matter, and is concentrated in living things.

Pranayama: The science of controlling the breath for increasing the effectiveness of meditation and exercises.

Pressure points: Places on the human anatomy with high levels of electrical conductivity. They tend to be located in neuro-muscular junctions, in the joints, or where bones lie close to the skin along a meridian.

Referred Pain: Pain generated in one area of the body but felt in another.

Shiatsu: A Japanese form of acupressure which uses various finger pressure massage techniques on points along the meridians.

Spinal Column: The backbone, composed of a series of bones called vertebrae, which are stacked on top of one another.

Stress: Tensions which tend to disturb the body's natural balance when internalized.

Tai Chi Chuan: A traditional Chinese system of movement which enables the body to balance and develop inner strength and vitality.

Tonic Point: An acupressure point that invigorates the whole system.

Visualization: A creative process of forming images and thoughts which positively directs one's life for obtaining greater energy.

RECOMMENDED READING

Academy of Traditional Chinese Medicine. *An Outline of Chinese Acupuncture.* Peking: Foreign Languages Press, 1975.

Ballentine, Rudolph M. (Editor). *Science of Breath.* Glenview, Illinois. The Himalayan International Institute of Yoga Science and Philosophy of U.S.A., 1977.

A *Barefoot Doctor's Manual.* Prepared by the Revolutionary Health Committee of Hunan Province. Seattle, Washington: Cloudburst Press, 1977.

Bean, Roy E., M.D. *Helping Your Health with Pointed Pressure Therapy.* West Nyack, New York: Parker Publishing Company, 1975.

Beau, Georges. *Chinese Medicine.* New York, New York: Avon Books, 1972.

Bendix, G. *Press Point Therapy.* New York, New York: Avon Books, 1976.

Brena, Steven F., M.D. *Yoga and Medicine.* New York, New York: Penguin Books, 1973.

Brodsky, Greg. *From Eden to Aquarius.* New York, New York: Bantam Books, 1974.

Chang, Stephan. *Complete Book of Acupuncture.* Millbrae, California: Celestial Arts, 1976.

Chao, Pi Chen. *Taoist Yoga.* Translated by Ku'an Yu Lu. New York, New York: Weiser, 1970.

Cannon, Walter B., M.D. *The Wisdom of the Body.* New York, New York: W.W. Norton and Company, 1963.

Carter, Mildred. *Helping Yourself with Foot Reflexology.* West Nyack, New York: Parker Publishing Company, 1969.

Chen, Ronald. *The History and Methods of Physical Diagnosis in Classical Chinese Medicine.* New York, New York: Vantage Press, 1969.

Feldenkrais, Moshe. *Awareness through Movement: Exercises for Personal Growth.* New York, New York: Harper & Row, 1972.

Gach, Michael. *Acu-Yoga.* Tokyo, Japan: Japan Publications; Harper & Row, Distributor, 1981.

Gach, Michael. *The Bum Back Book.* Berkeley, California: Celestial Arts, 1985.

Geba, Bruno. *Breathe Away Your Tension: An Introduction to Gestalt Body Awareness Therapy.* New York, New York: Random House, 1974.

Haas, Elson, M.D. *Staying Healthy with the Seasons.* Berkeley, California: Celestial Arts, 1981.

Heroldova, Dana. *Acupuncture and Moxibustion* (2 Volumes). Prague Academia, 1968.

Inayat Khan, Hazrat. *The Book of Health.* London, England: Sufi Publishing Company, 1974.

Inayat Khan Hazrat. *Practice of Sufi Healing.* New York, New York: Rainbow Bridge, 1977.

Jackson, Mildred, N.D., and Teague, Terri. *The Handbook of Alternatives to Chemical*

Medicine. Berkeley, California: Book-people, 1975.

Kloss, Jethro. *Back to Eden*. New York, New York: Lancer Books, 1971.

Krippner, Stanley and Villoldo, Alberto. *The Realms of Healing*. Berkeley, California: Celestial Arts, 1976, 1986.

Kundalini Research Institute. *Kundalini Yoga: Exercise and Meditation Manual*. Claremont, California: K.R.I. Publications, 1976.

Kushi, Michio. *The Teachings of Michio Kushi*. Boston, Massachusetts: East-West Foundation, 1972.

Langre, Jacques de. *Second Book of Do-In*. Magalia, California: Happiness Press, 1974.

Lappe, Frances Moore. *Diet for a Small Planet*. New York, New York: Ballantine, 1975.

Lawson-Wood, Denis and Lawson, Joyce. *The Five Elements of Acupuncture and Chinese Massage*. Rustington, England: Health Science Press, 1965.

Leadbeater, C.W. *The Chakras*. Adyar, Madras 20, India: Theosophical Publishing House, 1969.

Lu, K'uan-Yu. *Secrets of Chinese Medicine*. New York, New York: Weiser, 1964.

Mann, Felix, *Acupuncture, The Ancient Chinese Art of Healing*. New York, New York: Random House, 1962.

Mason, L. John, Ph.D. *Guide to Stress Reduction*. Berkeley, California: Celestial Arts, 1986.

Masunaga, Shizuto. *Zen Shiatsu*. Tokyo, Japan: Japan Publications, 1977.

Miller, Emmett E., M.D. *Self Imagery: Creating Your Own Good Health*. Berkeley, California: Celestial Arts, 1986.

Muramoto, Noboru. *Healing Ourselves*. New York, New York: Avon Books, 1973.

Nutrition Search, Inc., *Nutrition Almanac*. New York, New York: McGraw-Hill Company, 1975.

Ohsawa, George. *Acupuncture and the Philosophy of the Far East*. Boston, Massachusetts: The Order of the Universe Publications (Box 203, Prudential Center Station).

Oki, Masahiro. *Healing Yourself Through Okido Yoga*. Tokyo, Japan: Japan Publications, 1977.

Palos, Stephan. *The Chinese Art of Healing*. New York, New York: Bantam Books, 1972.

Ray, Sondra. *Celebration of Breath*. Berkeley, California: Celestial Arts, 1983.

Samuels, Mike, M.D. and Bennett, Hal. *The Well Body Book*. New York, New York: Random House, 1975.

Serizawa, Katsusuke, M.D. *Massage: The Oriental Method, Tsubo: Vital Points for Oriental Therapy*. Tokyo, Japan: Japan Publications, 1976.

Stevens, John O. *Awareness: Exploring, Experimenting, Experiencing*. Lafayette, California: Real People Press, 1971.

Teeguarden, Iona. *The Acupressure Way of Health*. Tokyo, Japan: Japan Publications, 1978.

Teeguarden, Ron. *Tonic Herbs*. Tokyo, Japan: Japan Publications, 1985.

Thomson, Judi. *Healthy Pregnancy the Yoga Way*. Garden City, New York: Dolphin Books, Doubleday & Company 1977.

Thie, John F. *Touch for Health*. Marina Del Ray, California: De Vorss & Company, 1973.

Todd, Mabel Elsworth. *The Thinking Body*. New York, New York: Dance Horizons Republications, 1959.

Wallnofer and von Rottauscher. *Chinese Folk Medicine*. New York, New York: Crown Publishers, 1971.

INDEX

ABOUT THE AUTHOR

MICHAEL REED GACH is the founder and director of the Acupressure Institute in Berkeley, California. Gach (pronounced like Bach) received his B.A. in Social Relations from Immaculate Heart College and is currently working on his Ph.D. in Acupressure Health Care at Columbia Pacific University. He has held an elementary teaching credential and currently holds a community college credential in Health, Physical Care Services and Related Technologies.

Gach is the author of *The Bum Back Book* and *Acu-Yoga: Self-Help Techniques for Relieving Stress and Tension*. Over ten years of research enabled Gach to originate a self-help stress management system incorporating acupressure and yoga postures. His *Acu-Yoga* book (published by Japan Publications, distributed by Harper & Row), is in its fourth printing, and has been translated into German and Spanish.

As an internationally recognized authority on finger pressure therapeutics, Gach leads seminars and workshops throughout the United States for various organizations, corporations, hospitals, colleges and special groups. Gach teaches workshops on how to relieve headaches, cramps, shoulder and neck tension, back pain, sports injuries, and ways to increase vitality. He also teaches seminars on the acupressure face lift and special classes showing how to use acupressure for weight loss.

Michael Gach has appeared on over 100 television and radio shows and has personally taught over 40,000 people during the past ten years. He is currently producing acupressure video and cassette tapes, writing booklets, flash cards, charts and other educational materials for distribution and as instructional aids in the training programs at his school and for home use.

The Acupressure Institute offers comprehensive, certified training programs in acupressure therapy, massage and teacher training. The school is fully approved by the California State Superintendent of Public Education, Department of Education and the Board of Registered Nurses for continuing education credits. For more information about acupressure training, books and charts, or having Michael Gach teach a special workshop in your town, contact the Acupressure Institute, 1533 Shattuck Avenue, Berkeley, CA 94709, (415) 845-1059.

Books and Cassettes
Available from the Acupressure Institute

• Books

Greater Energy at Your Fingertips
$8.95 plus $1.50 each for handling &
shipping.

The Bum Back Book
$7.95 plus $1.00 each for handling &
shipping.

Acu-Yoga: Self Help Techniques
$14.95 plus $1.50 each for handling &
shipping.

Acupressure for Health Professionals
(booklet) Important points for relieving
common ailments, 28 pages
$4.95 plus $1.00 for handling & shipping.

• Flash Cards

Acupressure Flash Cards
(30 points illustrated)
$5.95 plus $1.00 for handling & shipping.

• Cassette Tapes

Greater Energy in Ten Minutes
$9.95 plus $1.00 each for handling &
shipping.

The Bum Back Audio Cassette
$9.95 plus $1.00 for handling & shipping.

Acu-Yoga Exercise Cassette Tape
$9.95 plus $1.00 for handling & shipping.

• Video Tapes

Greater Energy at Your Fingertips Video
$39.95 includes shipping.
Available in Spring, 1988

The Bum Back Video
$39.95 includes shipping

Releasing Shoulder & Neck Tension
$39.95 includes shipping

Fundamentals of Acupressure
Course video & booklet
$45.00 includes shipping

Zen Shiatsu Video
$39.95 includes shipping

Free Literature

List of recommended books.
Gift/Product brochure.

Acupressure
Career Training

Approved by the Superintendent of Public Instruction, California State Department of Education

This one month intensive (150-hour) training program, originated by Michael Reed Gach, offers a comprehensive study of various finger pressure point methods and natural health care practices. To receive further information, fill out the following form and send to the address below.

Please send:

____ Brochure of Acupressure classes offered (free)

____ School catalogue and application form(s) for the Acupressure Massage Certification program (free)

____ Brochure(s) on the 1,000-hour Acupressure Therapy Program for professional practitioners and teacher training, $2 each

____ Information on coordinating Acupressure Workshops for groups of 20 or more people in my local area

I am interested in the following:
- ☐ Child Education
- ☐ Women's Health
- ☐ Bodywork
- ☐ Beauty (Spas, Salons)
- ☐ Pain Management
- ☐ Psychology/Counseling
- ☐ Sports Medicine
- ☐ Stress Management
- ☐ Traditional Chinese Medicine
- ☐ Advanced Acupressure Techniques

☐ Other interests _____

Be specific about interests noted above:

_____

_____

Name _____

Address _____

City & State _____

Zip _____

Phone (Day) _____

(Evening) _____